Kenneth E Berg

Hermann Kessler

Salt Water
Flies

J. B. Lippincott Company
Philadelphia and New York

SALT WATER FLIES

*Popular Patterns
and How to
Tie Them*

by
Kenneth E. Bay
and
Hermann Kessler

U.S. Library of Congress Cataloging in Publication Data

Bay, Kenneth E   birth date
    Salt water flies;
        1. Flies, Artificial. I. Kessler, Hermann, birth date
joint author.   II. Title.
SH451.B34   799.1/6   72-6109
ISBN-0-397-00939-9

Contents

Color Illustrations following page 134

Eight Featured Flies

Nine Classics

Introduction

When this book was planned, we knew that our material would have to be uncovered from many widespread sources. However, we did not realize our wealth of friends, who not only encouraged us but added their tributes to promote the sport of salt water fly fishing and the craft of fly tying. Of these, we are especially grateful to Bernard "Lefty" Kreh and Mark Sosin, for their enthusiastic encouragement and their appraisal of many veteran salt water fly fishermen whom they have met in their wide travels and whose work has not been properly recorded. We hope hereby to do credit to their names and their efforts.

An early work, if not the earliest, found in the library of Walter Burr of Storrs, Connecticut, is titled *Fly Fishing in Salt and Fresh*

Water and was published in London by John Van Voorst in 1851. In it are some highly imaginative hand-colored plates of "sea flies," showing the contemporary fly tyers' use of exotic materials, some of which are no longer available. The flies illustrated in this book are recommended for pollack, bass, mullet, and perch. The writer attests to the success of these flies and gives some pointers and illustrations for rigging the terminal tackle for them.

Approximately one hundred years later, in 1950, in his book *Salt Water Fly Fishing*, Joseph W. Brooks, Jr., wrote, "There is as yet no book available that lists salt water fly patterns." He is one of the many friends who encouraged us to develop the subject.

Although there are records from 1875 through 1920 of salt water fly fishing, no one seems to have indicated any specific patterns for the fish caught. In general, salmon and bass flies were adapted to salt water fishing. Only after 1920 did fishermen begin to record a preference in flies. Tom Loving, who fished in Chesapeake Bay, was the first to design a big white bucktail for striped bass, according to Joe Brooks in his *Salt Water Game Fishing*. From then on, other names appear—Homer Rhode, Jr., Howard Bonbright, Harvey Flint, Harold Gibbs, H. J. Greb—all of whom designed patterns based on their fishing experiences in various coastal waters.

One day, in reply to a letter of inquiry, Col. Joseph D. Bates, Jr., wrote me that there was a need for an informative book on popular salt water flies. When I mentioned this to a friend, Hermann Kessler, he said, "Let's do it!" He already had published the book *Fly-Tying* with his wife, Helen Shaw, and his creative abilities in design and photography and his years of experience as Art Director of *Field and Stream* magazine have made our collaboration a stimulating experience.

Seasoned salt water fly fishermen and salt water fly tyers along the East and West coasts not only gave us valuable information but told us what salt water patterns were popular in their areas and how they were tied.

We wish to express our particular gratitude to Al Brewster and his Rhody Fly Rodders of Rhode Island and to Dan Blanton and Bob Edgley of San Jose, California; also, to Myron Gregory of Oakland, California, to Charles F. Waterman of Deland, Florida, and to J. Edson Leonard of Rhode Island for their generous contributions of unique and innovative flies and for related material and anecdotes that are an integral part of this work.

As for myself, when my father thought I was old enough he took me fishing to the trout streams and bass lakes of Connecticut. As I grew to appreciate the subtleties of fresh water fly fishing, I learned to tie the flies with which to fish, and the pleasure of the sport became more profound. When I moved to Long Island in later years, I found that the long stretch of beaches on the south shore, with their heavy surf, required a different approach than the quiet beaches and secluded coves of the north shore. Time and tides affect the schools of fishes found there; seasons and storms add their charms and challenges.

Thus a new interest within easy reach of home brought me a new band of friends who were eager to share their knowledge and experiences. I pass this on to you with my good wishes for a new start in an old craft—salt water fly tying.

April, 1972   Kenneth E. Bay

Joe Brooks
and the
Platinum Blonde

It is most fitting to start the fly-tying sequences with Joe Brooks'
favorite, the Platinum Blonde, and with a tribute to Joe from
Lefty Kreh.

There have been a few people fly fishing in salt water for more than
100 years, but it was Joe Brooks, more than any other man, who opened
this exciting new world of fishing to the average fisherman. Just after
World War II, Joe began to experiment seriously and write about salt
water fly fishing. The returning soldiers, starved for a chance to fish
again, read almost with disbelief Joe's reports of the accomplishments of
the pioneer fishermen with whom he fished.

Most of these early exploits with a fly rod took place in southern
Florida. But Joe wrote also of striped bass fishing in populated areas,
and of angling in Central America, Cuba, Bermuda, the Bahamas, and

many, many other places. He drove home the point, time and again, that any fresh water fisherman could successfully catch some of these fish with his bass or salmon tackle.

His pioneer work and his wonderful stories in both magazines and books devoted to the subject were infectious. He caught the first of many species ever taken on a fly—and many of the largest. A number of world records are held by him—and there will be more. He is generally credited with being the first fisherman to deliberately take a bonefish with a fly; and his stories in the national magazines created a whole new breed of fly fishermen, who sought his "gray ghost of the flats," as Joe so frequently called this magnificent game fish.

Joe would never keep a fishing secret; he shared his fishing talents, his friendship, and his soul with thousands of his angling friends. There is little doubt in most anglers' minds that Joe Brooks is the most revered and loved of any American fly fisherman.

He's been like a father to me and many other outdoor writers. We lean on him for advice, and no one's company pleases us more than Joe's. I have never spent an unpleasant moment with him.

Certainly, most of us who have written a great deal about salt water fly fishing, and preached its doctrine, regard Joe as the father of salt water fly fishing. Joe started doing all of this so long ago that his earliest books and magazine articles tell you how to fish in areas that have long since been lost to progress and pollution.

Two factors are vital to becoming proficient in salt water fly fishing: they are a speedy delivery of the fly, and an accurate presentation. No one does it better than Joe—he knows instinctively what the fish is going to do and puts the fly in the right place.

Joe is proud of being a founding member of the "Brotherhood of the Junglecock," an organization founded in 1940 that is devoted to teaching boys how to fish and tie flies and instilling in them the basics of good sportsmanship and conservation. From a letter of Joe Brooks' we learn the following:

I think that the Platinum Blonde which I use for striped bass, jack crevalle, spotted sea trout, channel bass, bonefish, and tarpon (the fly I designed more than twenty years ago) has proven the best all-around salt water fly I have ever used.

Bill Gallasch has been tying salt water flies for twenty years, and for twelve of those years has tied flies for me. The quality of his work never varies. The flies hold up and last for years because he puts into them only the best materials and workmanship and is continually trying for improvements. With many years of experience fishing the Chesapeake Bay for stripers and offshore for bluefish, and with more than ten years of experience on the Florida bonefish flats and tarpon waters, he designs his flies with practical fishing in mind, to meet the need of the angler: whether to float the fly on top, swim it in mid-water, or keep in touch with the bottom. Bill is one of our best salt water fly tyers.

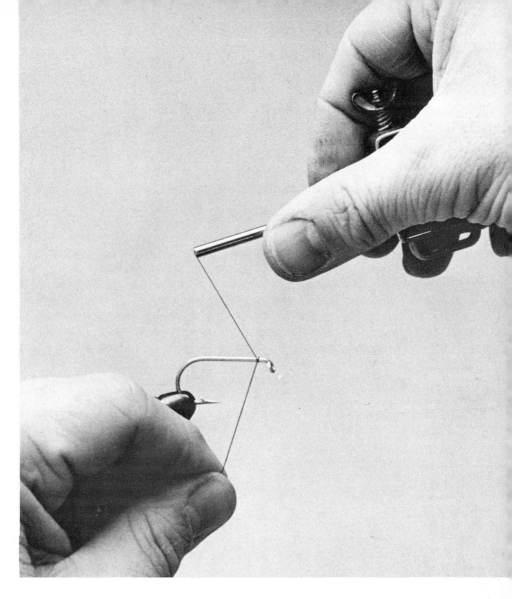

This is a white and silver fly, as its name implies, and is tied of natural white bucktail hair and silver Mylar. The Mylar will not tarnish in salt water or darken with age. After placing a No. 3/0 turned-down-eye hook in the vise, attach the tying thread (00 nylon is used here) a short distance behind the hook eye, as shown, by winding the thread over itself for a few turns, away from the eye. Continue to wind the thread down the hook shank with close, evenly spaced turns, stopping at the bend of the hook.

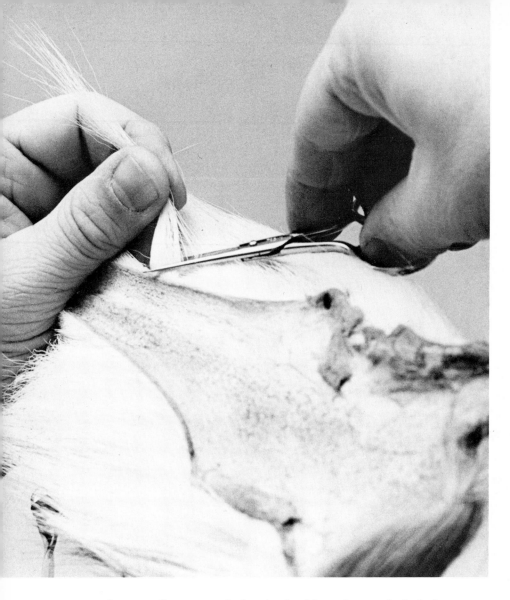

Cut a small segment of white bucktail hair close to the hide for maximum length. The tail of the fly will be 2 inches long. However, the hair should be long enough to cover the hook shank as well.

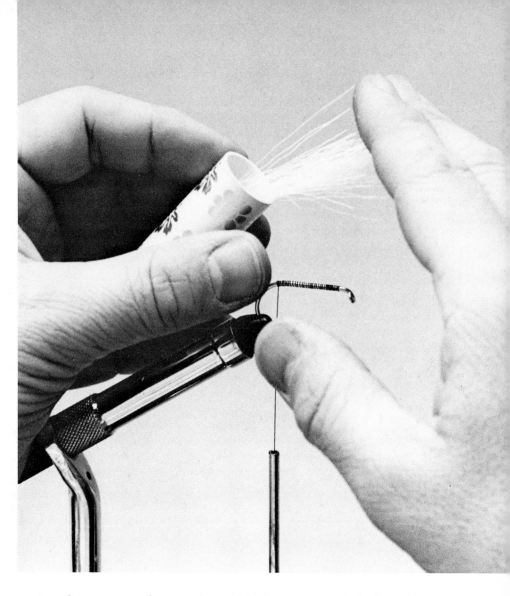

In order to even up the natural tips of the hair, you may find a lipstick case helpful. Drop the whole segment of hair into the case, with the tapered tips downward, and tap the case gently on the table.

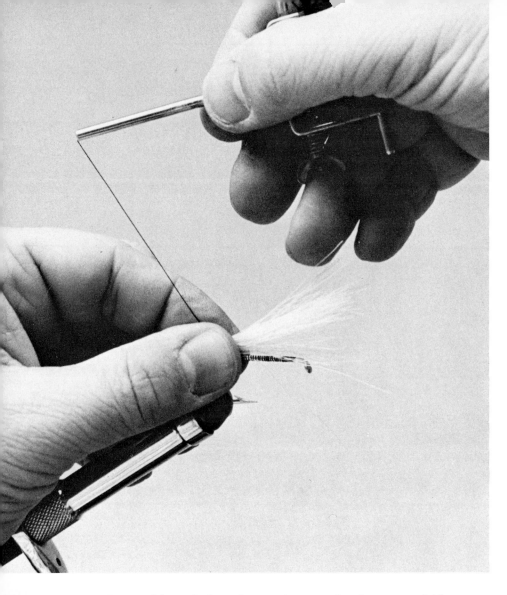

Removed from the lipstick case, the tapered ends are now fairly even, and the hair is ready for tying on the hook. Hold it firmly in position at the end of the hook shank, and bring the tying thread up between thumb and hair . . .

down between forefinger and hair on the far side of the hook . . .

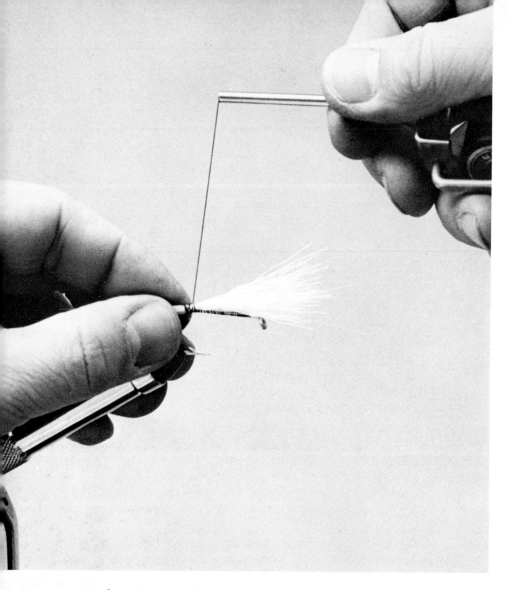

and repeat, to attach it securely to the top of the hook shank. Now work the thread toward the hook eye, binding down the bucktail hair to the top of the hook by holding it firmly in place for each turn of thread. A bit of lacquer applied to the hair as this is being done will keep the body from turning on the hook later on.

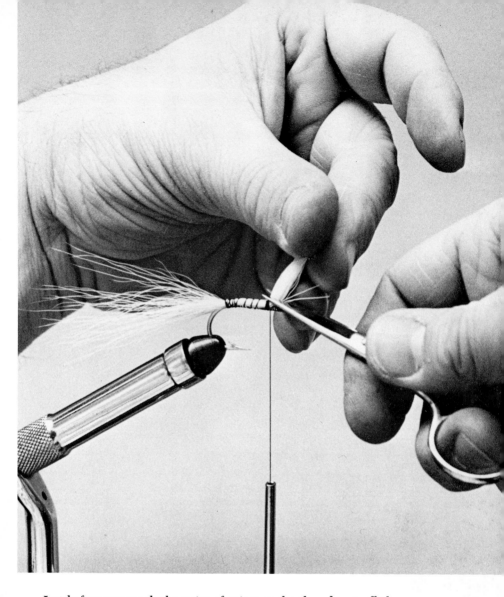

Just before you reach the point of tying on the thread, cut off the excess hair so as to leave the stub ends tapering down to the hook shank. Ample space remains for the head of the fly, and a smooth foundation has been made for the Mylar to cover.

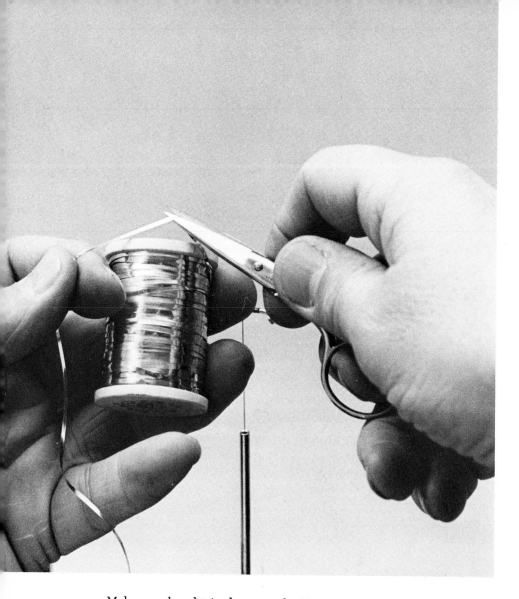

Mylar can be obtained on spools. Estimate a generous amount for covering the body with two layers of tinsel, approximately 7 to 9 inches.

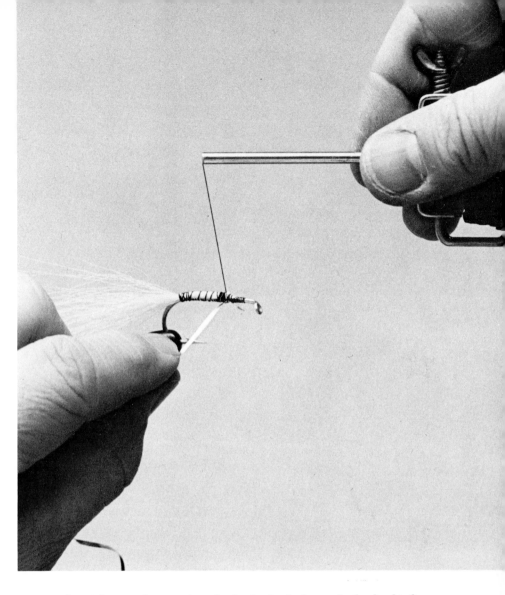

Tie the Mylar tinsel in against the hook shank, beneath the bucktail hair, as shown here. Several snug turns of tying thread may be used.

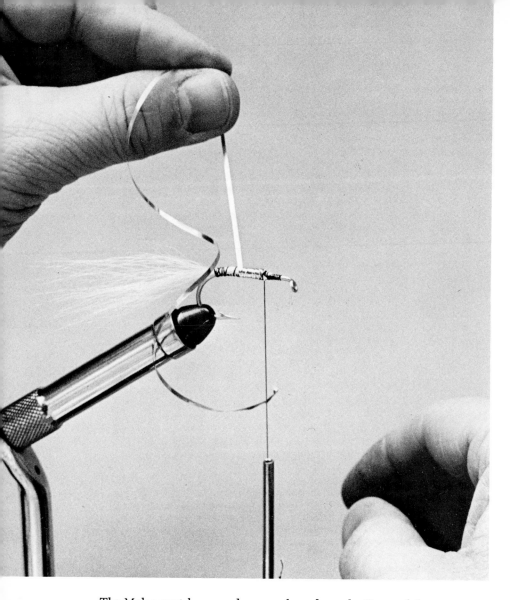

The Mylar must be wound on evenly and snugly. Be careful not to relax the tension while passing it from one hand to the other during the winding process.

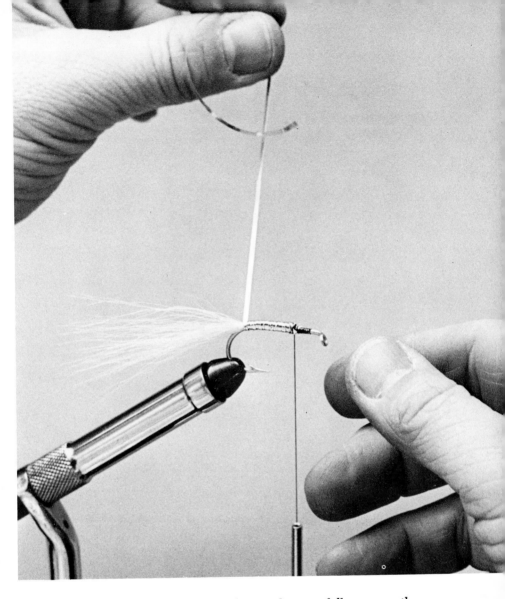

Having completed one layer of Mylar tinsel successfully, reverse the direction of winding and begin the second layer, working back toward the hook eye. Any unnecessary turns of overlapping tinsel at the tail will result in a pile-up of the Mylar, which can easily slip later on, loosening it along the entire body.

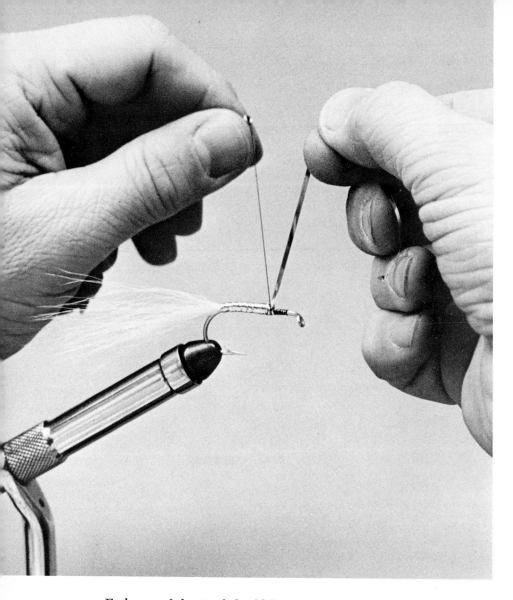

Each turn of the tinsel should lie neatly, edge to edge. With the two layers completed, bind the Mylar strand against the hook, still leaving room for the head.

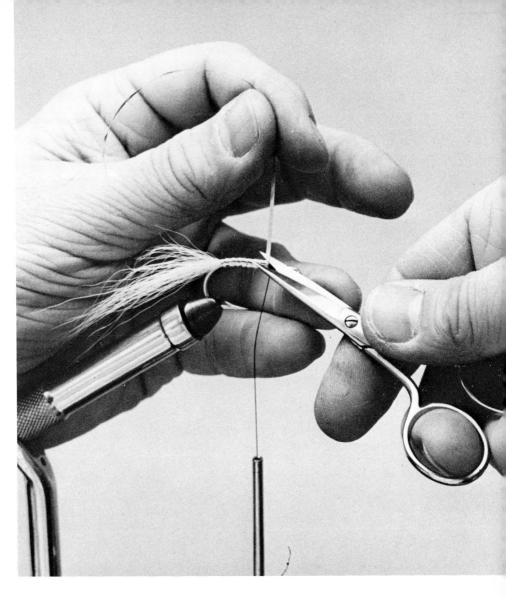

Snip off the tinsel close to the hook and bind down the cut end with a few turns of tying thread.

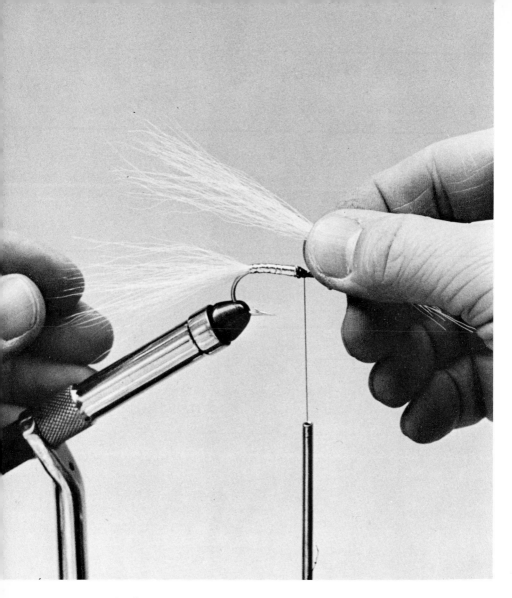

The fly is now ready for the wing, made from a segment of white bucktail, of approximately the same amount and length as the tail hair. The natural tips have been made fairly even by using the lipstick case again, as for the tail.

Holding the hair against the hook, as for the tail, bind the hair on at the forward end of the tinsel body.

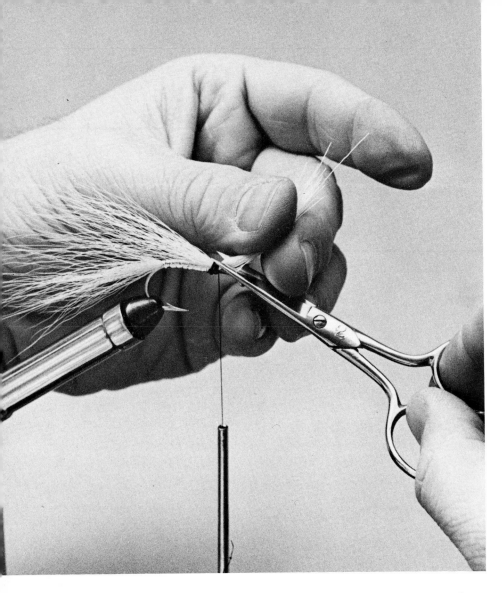

Slip all excess hair away in a long, even taper and bind it down to the hook, to form the head.

The wing should be raised slightly, so that it does not lie against the hook. One or two turns of thread wound tightly beneath it against the base of the hair will keep it cocked at the proper angle. Wrap the thread evenly over the cut ends of hair, forming a neatly tapered head, and complete it with the whip finish. Clip off the thread; do not break it.

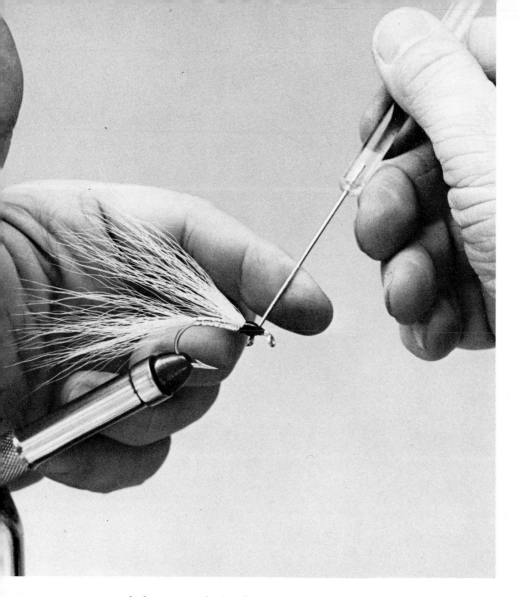

Apply lacquer to the head on all sides and allow to dry. Try to avoid getting lacquer in the hook eye. A second coat of lacquer will hide the thread.

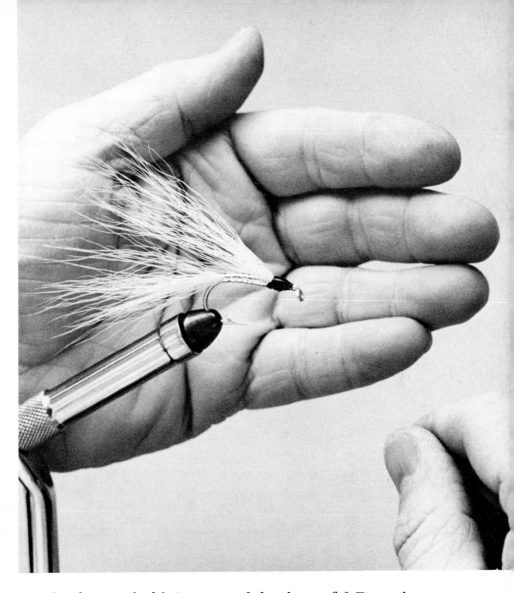

The Platinum Blonde! Are you satisfied with your fly? Tie another anyway.

Lefty Kreh
and the
Deceiver

Among the many admirers of Lefty Kreh is Mark Sosin, who has given us his appraisal of this vital and inspiring man.

Although he is probably best known for his unparalleled skill with a fly rod, Lefty Kreh ranks as one of the most knowledgeable and versatile anglers in the world today. There's hardly a gamefish species you can name in fresh water or salt that hasn't been the object of his attention at one time or another. Equally significant, Lefty Kreh fishes more in a single year than most anglers do in a decade. Friends frequently tell him that he has the most enviable career possible. He's a full-time professional outdoor writer and photographer, but for eight months of each year Lefty manages the largest fishing tournament in the world, where his responsibilities encompass spending more time on the water than at his desk. When the tournament is over each year, his personal travels take him to the far corners of fishingdom, where he gains additional experience and gathers material for his writings.

Lefty Kreh has been called a fisherman's fisherman because he is a master at the practical aspects of the sport. Theory is one thing, but if an idea can't be proven in practice you won't find Lefty touting it. Aside from his other multifaceted endeavors, Lefty Kreh serves as a consultant in the design and development of all types of fishing tackle. Many of the finest fly rods available, for example, are his original designs.

There are many who will attest to the fact that his desire and willingness to share his knowledge with others is his most salient attribute. Lefty Kreh has no secrets when it comes to fishing. Thousands of delighted people point to Lefty as the man who taught them to flycast or showed them a technique that was new. He has been a professional fly tyer and has developed a number of exceptional patterns.

Throughout the year, Lefty conducts a multitude of fishing clinics all over the country. If you ask him a question, he'll work overtime to make certain you have the answer. His answers are generally in the form of a demonstration, or he will pull a felt-tip marker out of his pocket and diagram the response for you on the first available piece of paper he can lay his hands on.

Lefty Kreh's list of credits are extensive and impressive, but he seldom talks about them. The fact that he was elected a member of the Fishing Hall of Fame has little bearing on the fact that he is first and foremost a fisherman. And, if you can talk fishing, you're speaking Lefty Kreh's language.

Lefty has a favorite fly which he developed with these three points in mind: it must have a minimum of air resistance when cast, sink readily, and have the action of a swimming baitfish. His Deceiver is the result. When he is too busy to tie his own flies, he turns to his favorite salt water fly tyer, Chico Fernandez, about whom he says:

Chico is a perfectionist, and it shows in the materials he uses and the flies he makes. Great care is taken to get the proper shades of feathers, the right bucktail or calftail, and he uses the finest of stainless steel hooks. With it all, he is constantly searching for better supplies. . . . I always try to borrow Chico's flies when we fish together. I am sure-certain that the fish would rather select his than mine. Naturally, I always forget to return them.

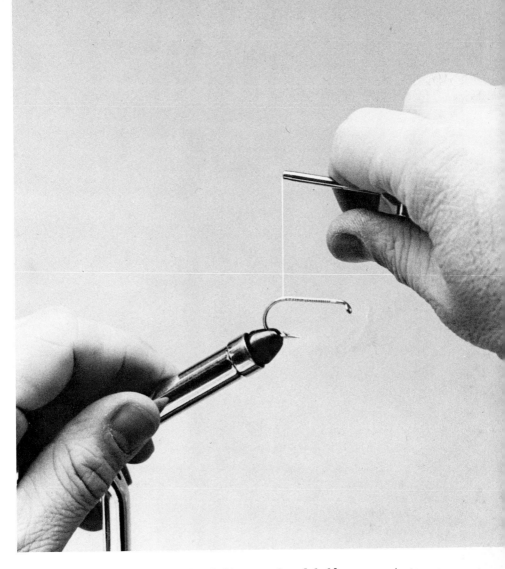

Many tyers find the use of a bobbin, or thread holder, convenient. Leave a small space behind the eye of the hook and attach the thread there. Wind it closely back to the bend, covering the hook completely. This provides a good friction base when other materials are tied on. The hook used here is a No. 3/0 tin-plated hook, turned-down eye.

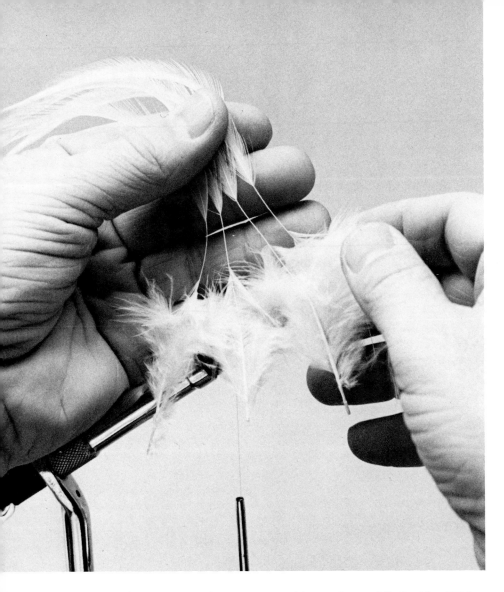

For the Deceiver, select two pairs of long white saddle hackles. With a hook of this size, the hackles should be approximately 4 to 4½ inches long. Strip off the webby portion, freeing the quills for tying on.

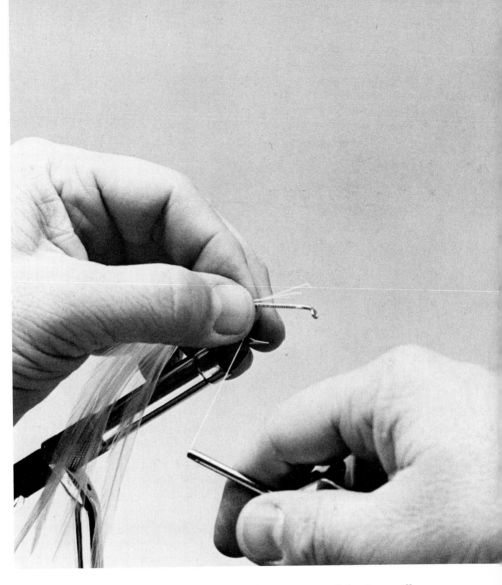

Grasp the hackles in such a way that the two pairs of feathers will curve toward each other to form a single tail. Feathers in this position will have an undulating movement in the water. Hold them ready for tying on the hook where the winding ended.

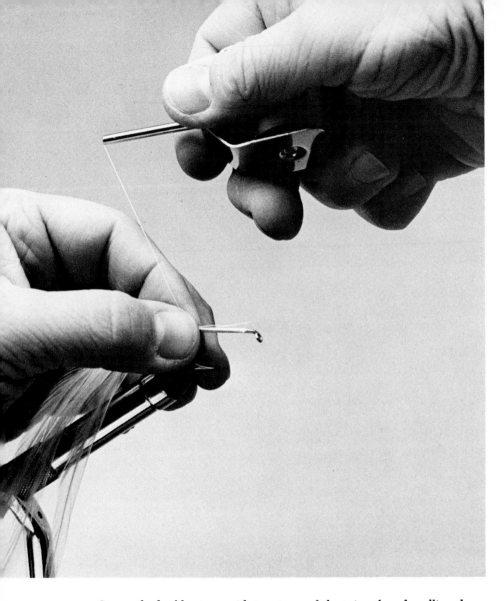

Secure the hackle stems with two turns of the tying thread, pulling the thread back between thumb and forefinger before bringing it downward each time. This will keep the stems on top of the hook. A few more turns of thread along the stems away from the bend of the hook, and then back again, will hold the stems, and the stubs can be trimmed away. Wind the thread along the hook toward the eye.

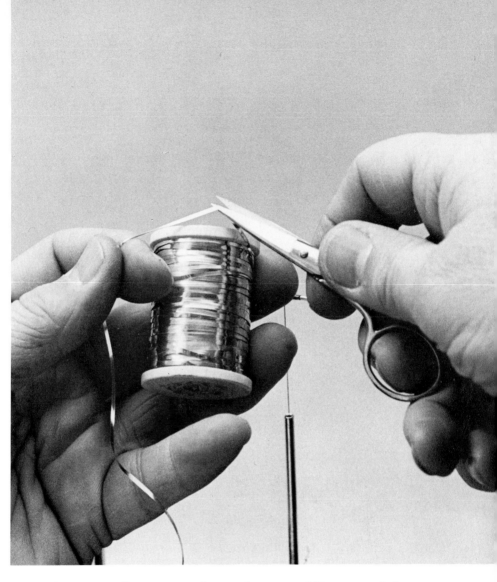

Mylar, an excellent nontarnishing, silvery, tinsel-like material, has found great acceptance among salt water fly tyers as a substitute for the metallic tinsel used for traditional salmon and fresh water flies. Here it measures about 1/32 inch in width. For this pattern you will need a piece of sufficient length to cover the hook twice—about 9 inches.

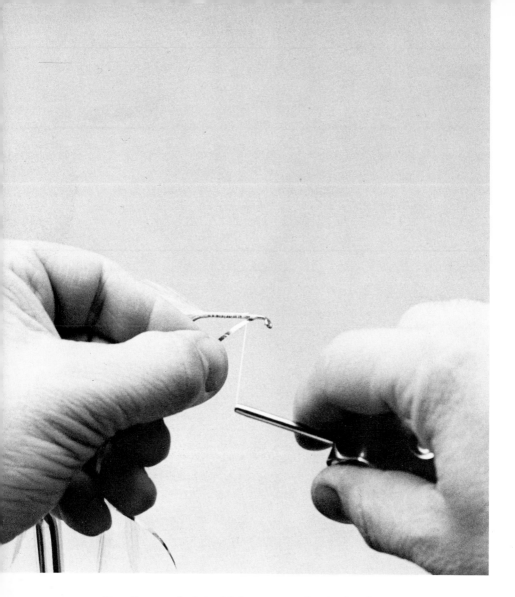

Cut off one end of the Mylar at an angle which will leave a long point. Hold the end of the point underneath the hook shank and secure it with a few turns of thread. Leave the bobbin hanging; both hands are needed for wrapping the tinsel. Coat the hook shank with lacquer and wind on the tinsel before the lacquer has dried.

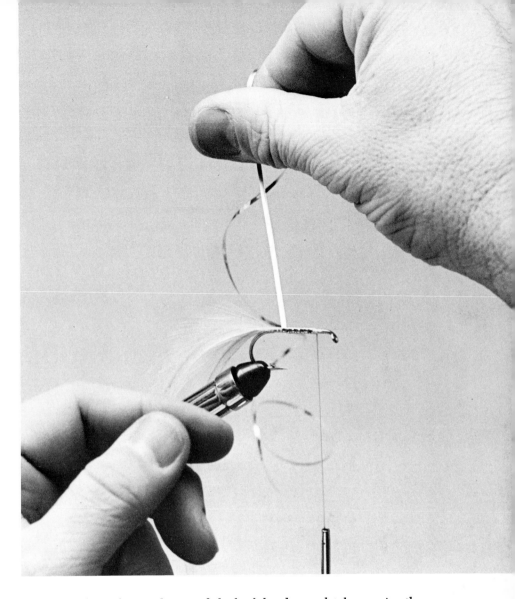

Wrap the Mylar evenly toward the hook bend, completely covering the thread base.

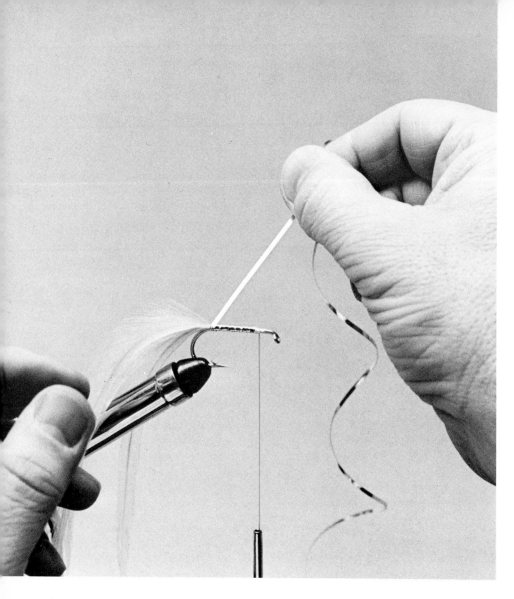

When you have reached the hook bend, reverse the direction of tying and wrap the Mylar evenly toward the hook eye, carefully covering the first layer. It is important that, upon reaching the bend of the hook, no extra turns are taken unless they are moving toward the hook eye. A buildup of tinsel in one position has a tendency to slide and loosen during fishing.

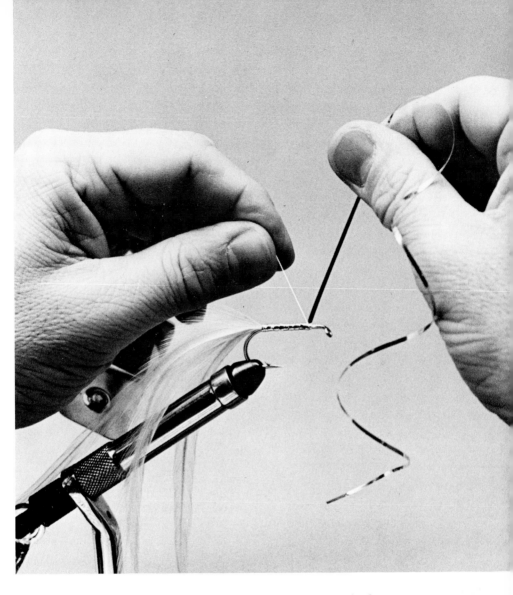

When the body is completely covered, do not make any further turns of tinsel but tie off where the tinsel was tied in. Cut off the excess.

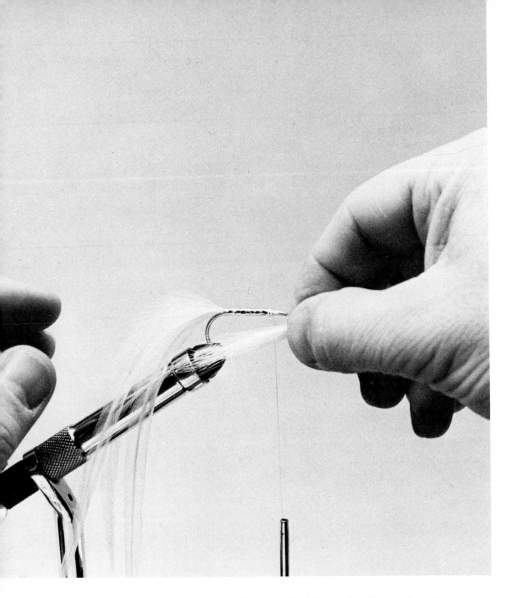

Select a small bunch of white bucktail hair of sufficient length to extend beyond the hook point and cover it. Measure against the hook and place it in the correct position with the right hand; then hold it there with the left hand, preparatory to tying in.

The bucktail hair must be tied underneath the hook shank. Grasp the bunch of hair tightly and hold it firmly while the first two turns of tying thread secure it to the underside of the hook.

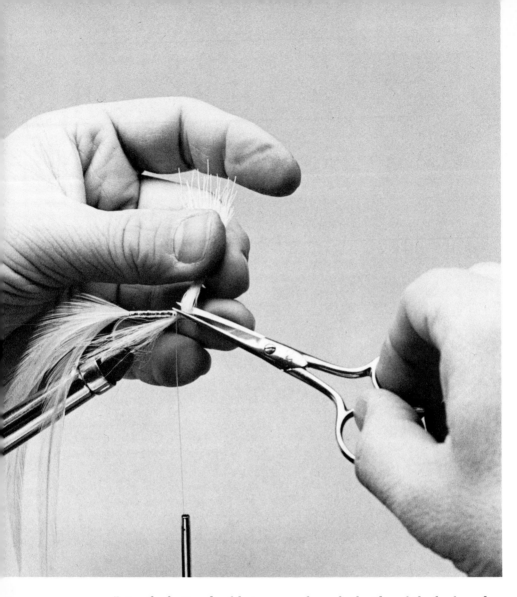

Bring the butt ends of hair up evenly on both sides of the hook, and make a few more wraps of thread across them before trimming away the excess hair. A few more turns of thread will cover the stubs.

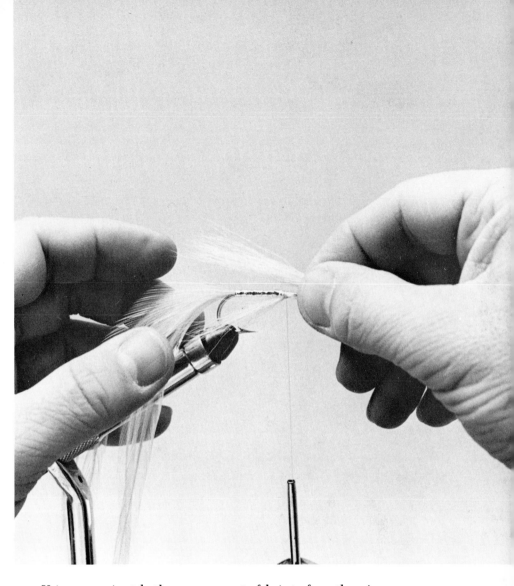

Using approximately the same amount of hair to form the wing, measure it against the hook for length. It should extend as far back as the lower tuft of hair.

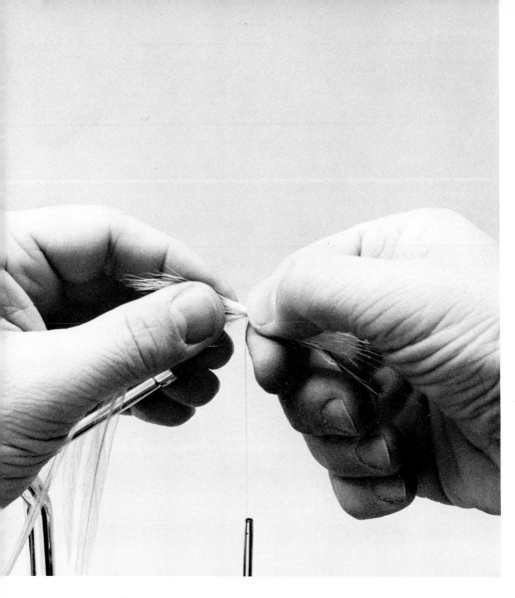

The wing should be tied on so that all of the hair remains on top of the hook, and the angle of the wing should mirror-match the angle of the hair beneath the hook. When the wing hair has been positioned by the right hand, hold it there with the left hand while it is being tied on.

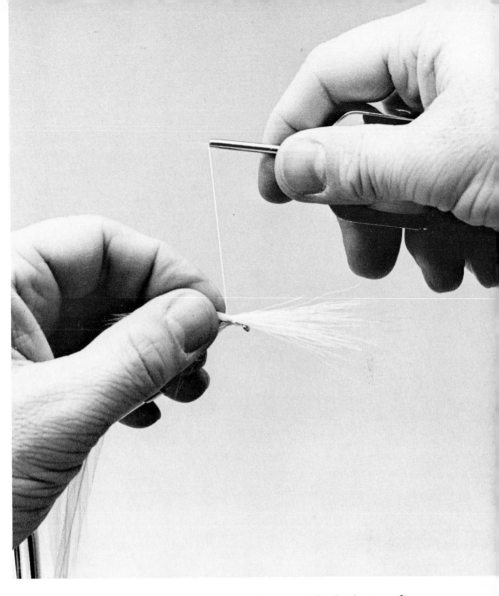

With the hair wing held tightly against the top of the hook, immediately above the lower tuft, bring the tying thread up and over it two or three times. The excess hair should be trimmed away and the stubs bound down to make a smooth profile.

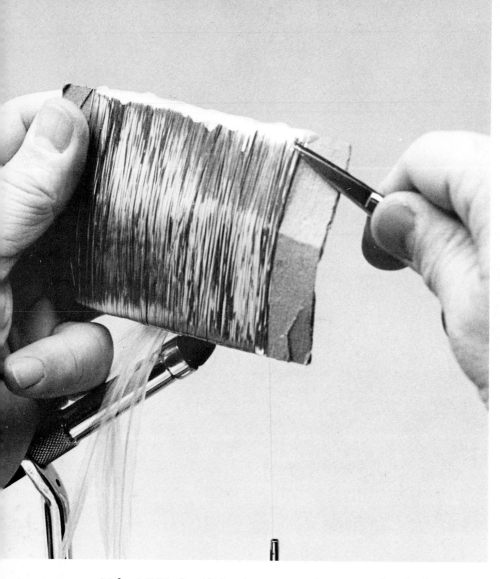

Mylar 1/64 inch wide has been wrapped over a card to facilitate cutting strips of it for use now. The upper edge of this card was coated with heavy glue to prevent the Mylar from unwinding when cut.

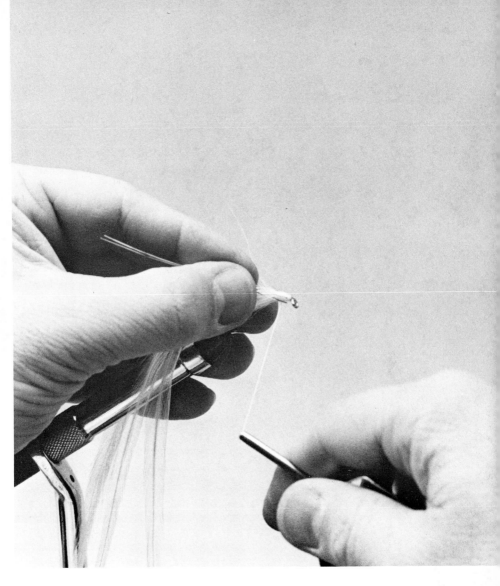

Tie in two strips of Mylar 2½ inches long on each side of the head. Each pair should be tied on so that the strips will stand slightly away from each other on the fly. Tie the strips as closely as possible to the side of the base, or widest part, of the head.

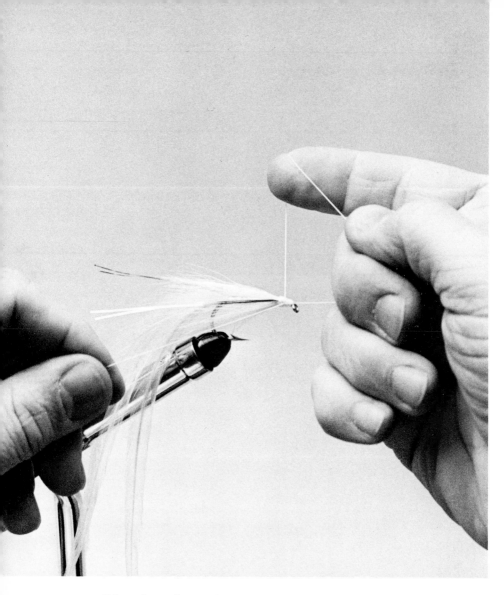

When the Mylar strips are in the proper horizontal position, parallel to the body, the head is wrapped so that the final form tapers down evenly toward the hook eye. The whip finish has almost been completed here. The vertical thread, held in the right hand, is wrapped around the head toward the eye, perhaps three or four more turns, after which the left hand pulls, the loop diminishes and closes completely, and the thread is cut off.

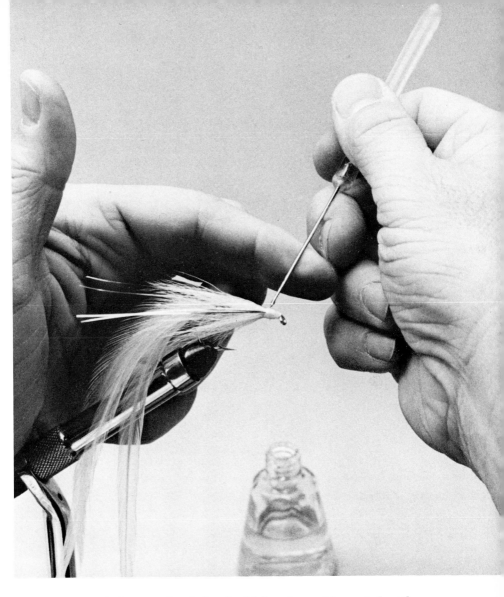

The head of the completed fly should be thoroughly coated with lacquer. This is clear lacquer, but many colors are popular. Lefty's sample of his Deceiver has a red head. A drop of clear lacquer over the red will give added depth and gloss.

Mark Sosin
and the
Blockbuster

We started this book with the concept that it would be by, for, and about sportsmen who look to salt water fly fishing as a growing sport. Therefore, we turned to Lefty Kreh for an appraisal of his friend and frequent fishing companion, Mark Sosin, whose name is familiar to readers of our national sports magazines.

Mark Sosin is a dynamic young man who, through his writing and lectures, has preached about the joys of salt water fly rodding to all who will listen.

Mark has been a full-time free-lance outdoor writer for many years. He is a superb fly fisherman; one of the best at fighting fish. He started his fly rod career fishing for striped bass and bluefish on Barnegat and the other bays of his home state of New Jersey. He has fished Africa,

Central and South America, and most of the North American continent, both in fresh and salt water.

There are many outdoor writers, but Mark is one of the exceptional few who can turn a good word, and he knows his tackle and techniques thoroughly. Mark can discuss and fish with anyone. He knows how to tear down and repair a reel, rig all the better-known knots, cast well, tie flies, or do any of the many chores that are required. He is a total salt water fly fisherman.

Mark was one of the men who got together some years ago in Toms River, New Jersey, to create the Salt Water Fly Rodders of America, the official organization that supervises the sport. Mainly because of this organization, salt water fly fishing has been brought before the general public, and order has come to the sport.

He has held the position of World Records' Editor for this organization since its inception, and in addition to overseeing the records he has established a few himself. Undoubtedly one of the greatest catches ever made on a fly rod—anywhere—is the 53-pound 6-ounce Allison tuna that he landed a few years ago offshore from Bermuda. The Allison tuna is regarded by those who fish with ocean tackle as one of the toughest fish in the sea. To catch one on a fly rod was an almost unthinkable act. Mark was successful on the first fish into which he sank a fly.

Mark Sosin is already well known to salt water fly fishermen, but in the years to come he will continue to contribute so much to the sport that it is almost certain he will be remembered as one of the "greats" in the field.

When we asked Mark for his favorite salt water fly and how it evolved, he told us:

My favorite pattern is fashioned from bucktail and Mylar and appropriately named the Blockbuster. It was designed on my bench with Bub Church at the vise and me over his shoulder. I told Bub what I wanted to accomplish, and we worked out the pattern together. Louis "Bub" Church has long been considered to be one of the finest and most creative fly tyers the angling world has ever seen. His knowledge of flies, fly tying, and fly fishing in both fresh water and salt water may be equaled but will never be surpassed. He is a master at innovation. People who visit Bub are constantly amazed to learn that he employed many of the techniques that we know so well today, before most fishermen knew anything about salt water fly rodding. You might talk to him about a "new" pattern and he'll show you flies he tied thirty years ago that are almost identical.

With the Blockbuster in a variety of colors Mark has taken striped bass, bluefish, dolphin, mackerel, small tarpon, bonefish, jacks, cobia, and tuna.

46

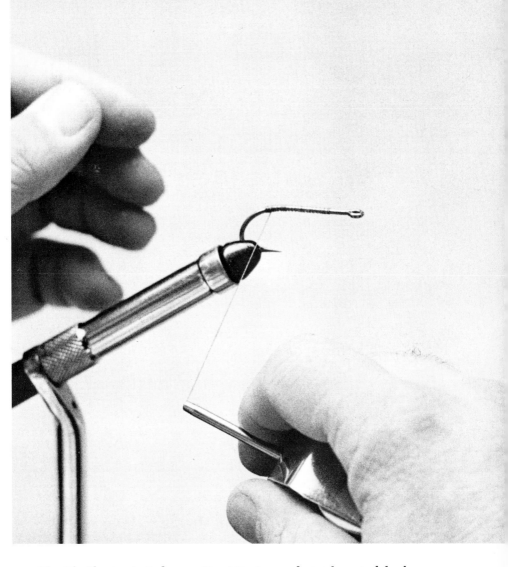

The Blockbuster is tied on a No. 1/0 ring-eyed stainless steel hook, and, since the tying thread will be exposed, forming the body of the fly, a maroon 00 nylon thread has been attached to the hook about a quarter of the length of the hook shank, behind the hook eye, and has been wound back along the shank to where the tail will be tied.

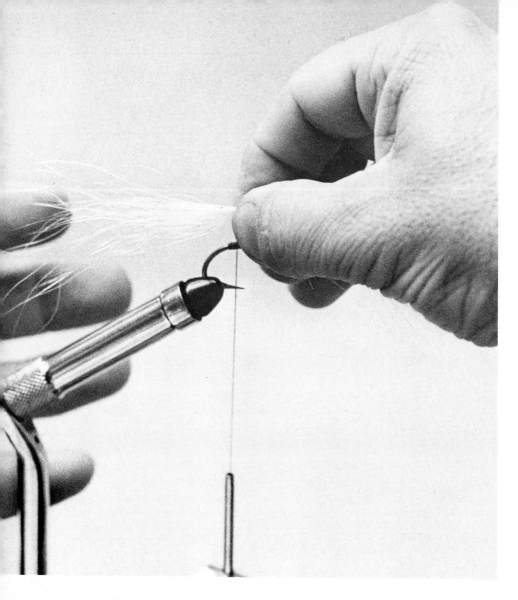

The tail, of white bucktail, should be approximately 2½ inches long. It may be tied on as it was removed, without making the naturally tapered tips even, and the clipped ends may be "blunt cut"—that is, not carefully trimmed to form a taper down to the hook shank.

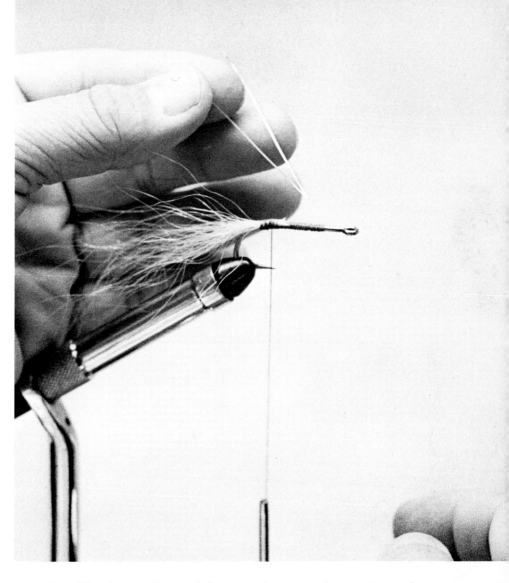

The tail has been tied on and the excess hair clipped away. A strand of 1/64-inch Mylar is added next. Cut the strand about 3½ inches long and fold in half. This has a double purpose.

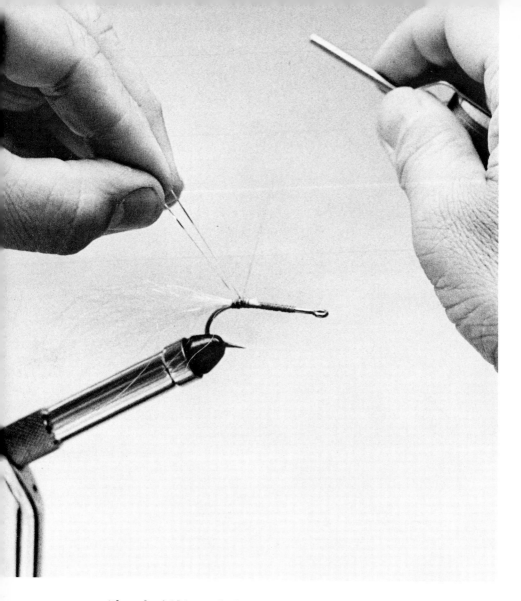

Place the fold beneath the hook, a strand on each side, and tie it there with the Mylar strands extending up and back toward the tail, thus preventing the Mylar from pulling out and automatically achieving strips of equal length on both sides of the fly.

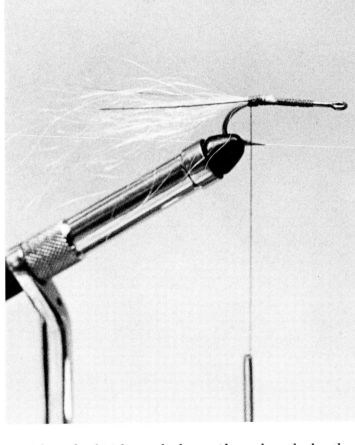

The ends of Mylar reach about midway along the length of the tail. Complete the first segment of the body by wrapping the tying thread forward, about ¼ inch, over the clipped ends of the tail.

You will be adding three more segments of white bucktail hair of approximately the same amount and length, each with its own strip of Mylar tied on in the same manner. Each segment of hair should overlap the butt of the preceding one, and all should be kept entirely on top of the hook.

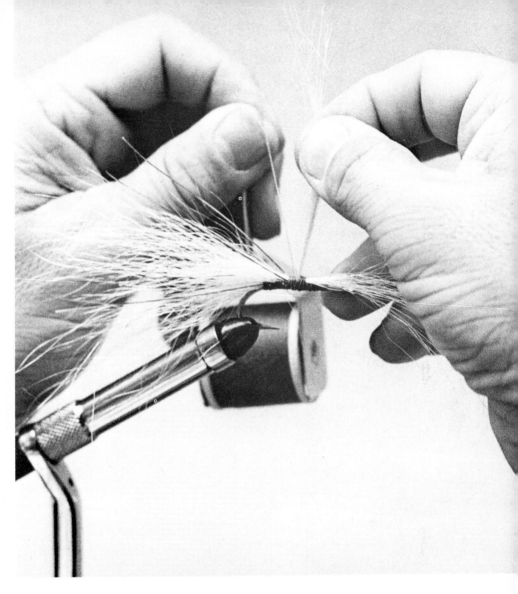

By not tapering the cut ends of the preceding section of hair, the overlapping of successive segments raises the hair above the horizontal. You can also make a few extra turns of thread at the point where the next section will be tied on, or you can pull the segment of hair upward and wind a few turns of tying thread tightly behind it, close to the base of the hair, as shown here. This second suggestion is preferable.

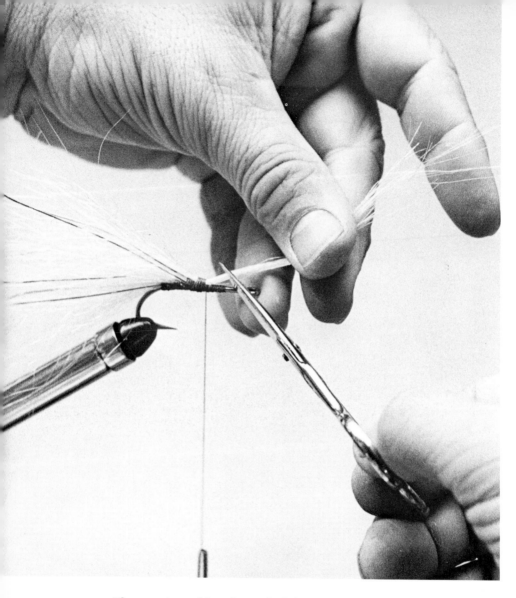

Three sections of hair forward of the tail are all the Blockbuster needs, and all sections should take up no more than about two thirds of the hook shank. Both the long hair, tied well back on the hook, and the angle at which it juts upward from the shank are necessary to prevent a "wrap-around" (the hair becoming caught in the bend of the hook).

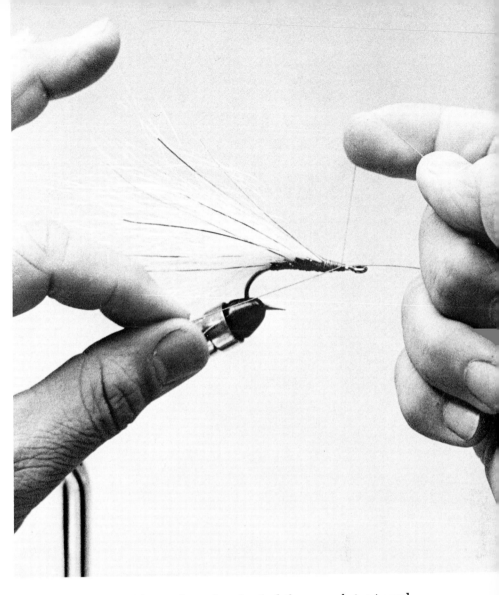

The last section of hair to be tied on has had the excess hair trimmed away in a long taper toward the hook eye. Wrapped smoothly with tying thread, it forms the slim tapered head. It is not necessary in this pattern to bring the long head all the way to the hook eye. Complete the tying with a whip finish.

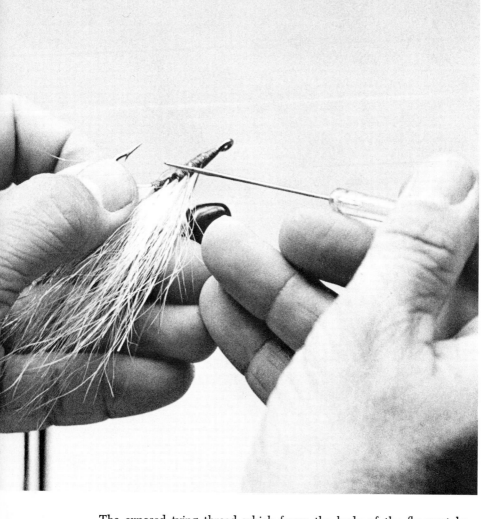

The exposed tying thread which forms the body of the fly must be protected. Several applications of clear epoxy cement over the thread will make it practically indestructible, and the coating will give brilliance to the maroon body. Let the epoxy harden between each application, and take care to keep it out of the hair.

The Blockbuster is now complete and ready for use anywhere in the world.

Stu Apte
and the
Tarpon Fly

A pilot for one of the international airlines is also one of our well-known "tarpon tamers." When he is not flying, he may be guiding. And when he is not guiding, he may be fishing for another world's record and then writing about it for his ever-increasing public.

We had a time tracking down information about this active man but, with the help of Joe Brooks, learned the following:

Stu Apte is a long-time fisherman. He has worked at it since he was a young lad, and he knows fishing and tackle thoroughly. I have known him for twenty years, and everything he does is thought out and worked out. Expert anglers agree that there is no excuse for tackle failure, and this is where Stu's interest and efforts have paid off for all fishermen. He has a complete knowledge of what it takes to hook and fight and land big, tackle-testing fish. He has experimented with knots, flies, and

59

tackle, especially for fly fishing, and his findings have been a great help to all anglers, as well as helping Stu himself to make some unbelievable, great catches.

Stu has named his favorite pattern the Apte Tarpon Fly. He prefers the red and yellow color combination because he believes that "this particular pattern . . . stirs the tarpon's memory of his favorite food, the palolo (red) worm." Ray Donnersberger, a proficient amateur tyer from Chicago, has produced a number of successful patterns which have deceived both tarpon and permit. Stu has proved this for the records.

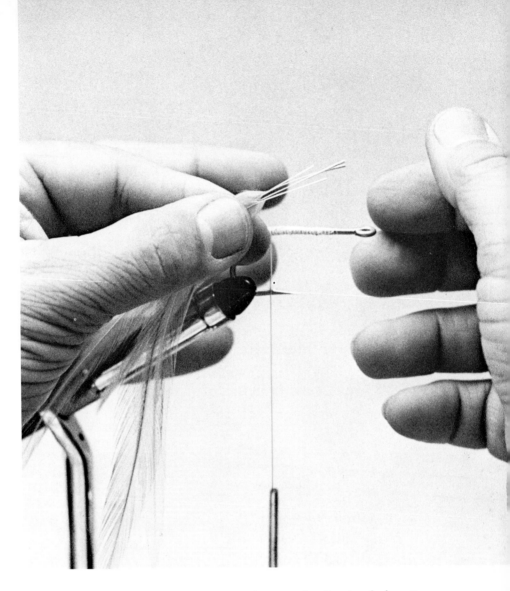

This simple yet extremely effective salt water fly, Stu Apte's favorite pattern, is constructed entirely of dyed saddle hackles and a No. 5/0 stainless steel hook with a ringed eye. Prepare two pairs of long saddle hackles for the tail to be tied on the hook with the glossy side of each feather turned inward—yellow for the two center feathers, red for the one on each side.

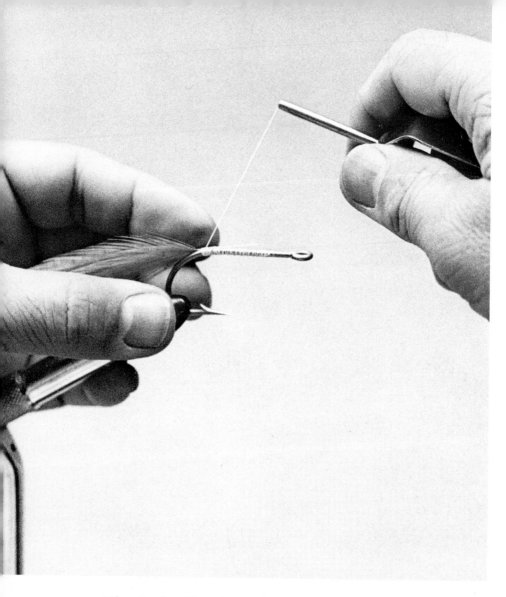

When the "good" or glossy sides of the feathers of each pair face inward, the result of their natural curve will be a spreading tail, which is desired for this streamer. Turn the cut ends of the quills back toward the tail and catch them with the tying thread before clipping off the remainder, to lock them in place.

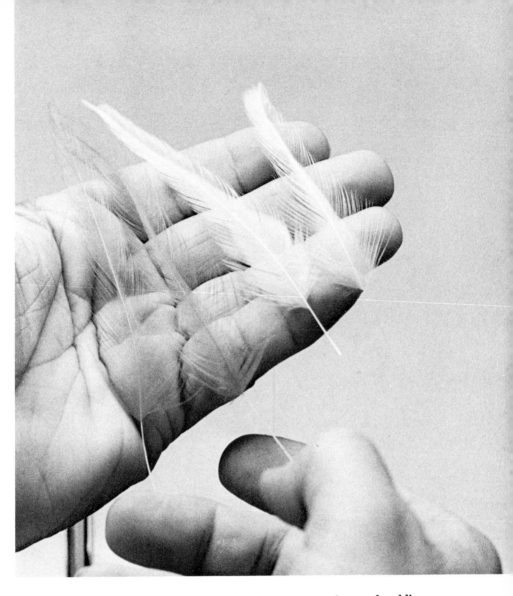

After the tail has been securely tied, select two more long red saddle hackles and two more yellow ones of about the same length. These will be wrapped on at right angles to the hook, as for a dry fly. The feathers should be at least as wide on either side of the quill, when the barbs have been spread, as the distance between hook shank and point. The amount of webby material along the quill is not particularly important.

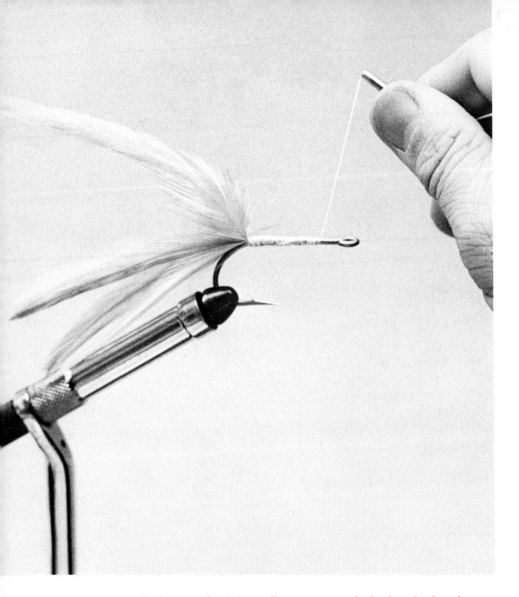

After the lower ends of the quills were stripped, the four feathers have been tied in with the colors alternating, red and yellow, with the glossy side toward the hook eye. By tying them on, as shown here, the feathers are in a good position to be wound around the hook.

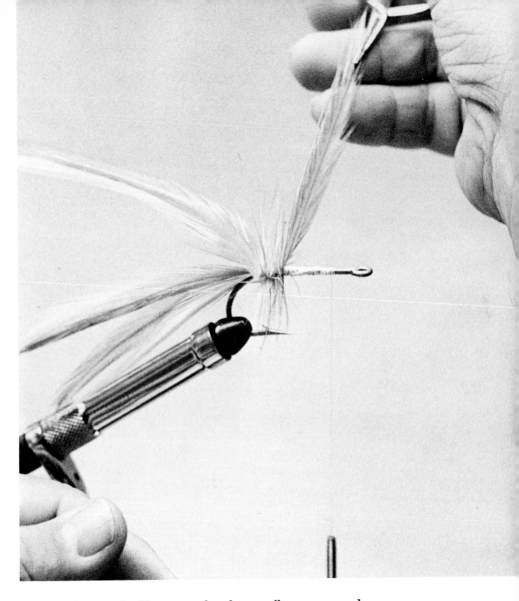

The first two hackles, one red and one yellow, are wound on as one.
The use of hackle pliers here may aid in keeping the two together.

Wind them toward the hook eye in an even but not closely spaced spiral, covering about ½ inch of the shank. Tie off the ends, being careful to keep an equal tension on both feathers.

Wind on the two remaining hackles, weaving them through the ones already there to make the distribution of hackle and color as even as possible.

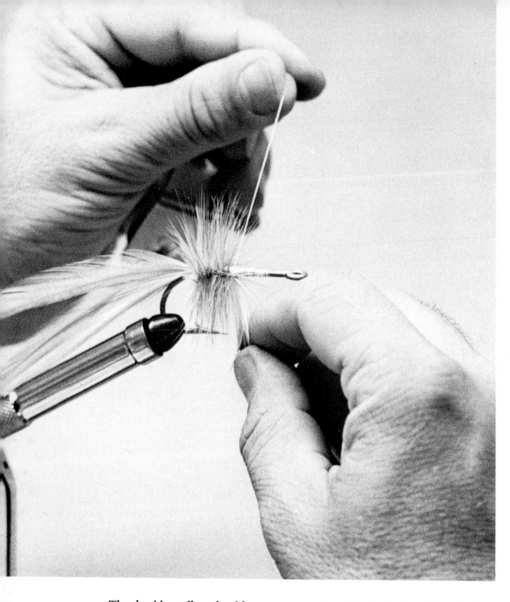

The hackle collar should cover approximately ½ inch of the hook shank next to the tail, not more. When you reach the end of the first two hackles, carefully secure the ends of the second two just in front of them. If you prefer to hold the two hackles with your fingers instead of with the pliers, do so. Just make sure the tension is equal on both hackles. Keep the thread taut at all times.

When the hackle is securely fastened and the excess cut away, it is a good precaution to use a wrap knot before covering the hook with two or three closely wrapped layers of tying thread, ending with the thread close to the eye. Another whip finish here will complete the fly.

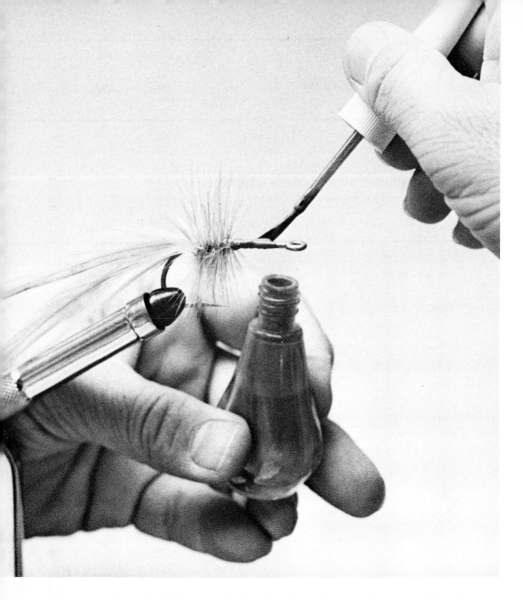

Coat all of the exposed thread with red lacquer, being careful to keep it out of the hackle, and when dry cover the lacquer with a clear coat of epoxy cement. If any of the hackle barbs have been bound down in tying, they can be gently raised by using a slim needle to release them.

Cap Colvin
and the
KaBoomBoom Popper

We turned to Mark Sosin again, for the following report:

When the history of salt water fly rodding is chronicled in detail, the name of Elwood "Cap" Colvin will be given a place of prominence. Cap, as he is lovingly known to all, has encouraged hundreds and perhaps thousands of anglers to try the light wand. For many years, Cap Colvin operated a tackle shop along the New Jersey coast, where he had already gained a reputation for his skill with spinning and conventional tackle. One day, long before most people ever dreamed of using a fly rod in salt water, Cap discovered the thrills of that type of fishing.

His home and shop were located on Island Beach, a narrow strip of land that separates the pounding surf of the Atlantic from the shallow waters of Barnegat Bay. This is striped bass and bluefish country, and Cap Colvin made the most of it. He fished daily in an untiring effort to

71

uncover the best methods of taking those species on fly and then shared that information with anyone willing to listen. And he would locate concentrations of fish, but instead of carefully guarding this secret Cap would excitedly send others to the location to share in the sport.

It didn't take long before fly rodders from all over the East flocked to his tackle emporium to sip coffee and talk at length about salt water fly rodding. At that time, fly rodding along the coast was in its infancy, and Cap's "cracker barrel" was the only place where information was readily exchanged. Somewhere along the way, Cap Colvin found that stripers and bluefish would clobber long fly rod poppers, so he sat down at his vise and created the now famous KaBoomBoom (named after the sound it made in the water). Shortly after that, Cap began exploring the possibilities of fishing the breaking surf with a fly rod, developing many of the techniques that others are following today.

Cap Colvin's contribution to salt water fly rodding didn't end there. Instead, he became one of the founders of the Salt Water Fly Rodders of America, an international organization of fly rod enthusiasts that now keeps the world records for salt water fly rod catches. Over the years, Cap Colvin served that organization in practically every capacity, including the presidency of the first official chapter in the country. Today, Cap Colvin has turned the reins of his tackle shop over to his son and has moved to Jensen Beach, Florida, where he is busily waging a continual war on the local fish population.

If you happen to be fishing the Jensen Beach area, you can recognize Cap Colvin easily. He's the only fisherman on the water who carries no other tackle in his boat except salt water fly rods.

Cap's friends never fail to look him up in Florida. When Nelson Bryant, the Outdoor Editor of *The New York Times*, makes his annual trek to the south, he is bound to call on Cap and get in one or two fishing trips.

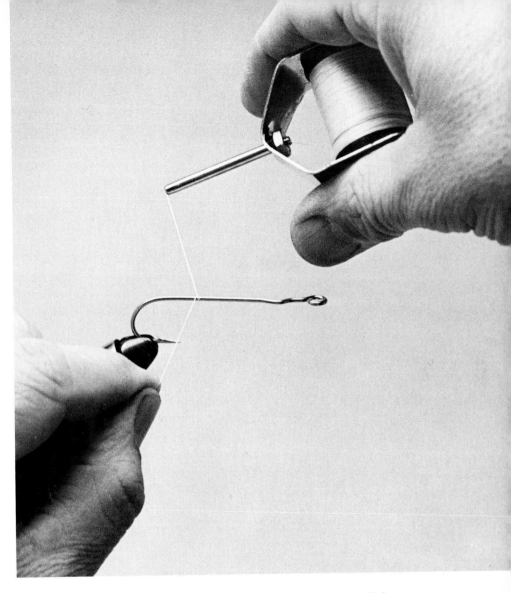

For this cork-bodied popper, use a No. 3/0 extra-long light-wire nickel-plated hook, with a kink which will prevent the cork body from turning on the hook. Since the finished popper will be white, use white thread for tying on the tail. This is the only actual "tying" that is done.

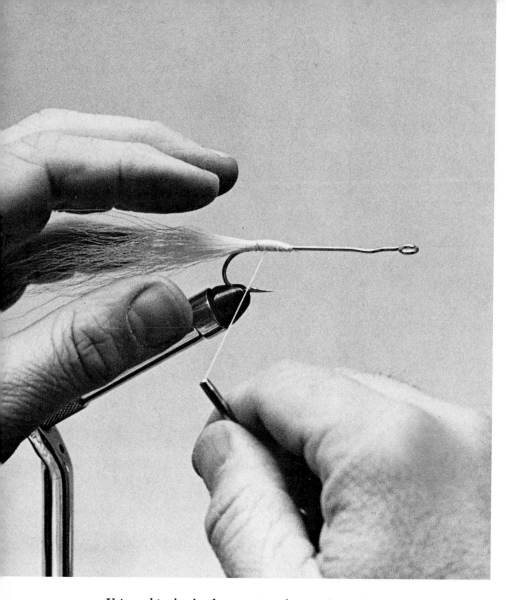

Using white bucktail approximately 3 inches in length, tie on the tail and bind down the clipped ends about ½ inch along the hook. Cover them with several layers of tying thread before applying the whip finish. This will form the very end of the popper body.

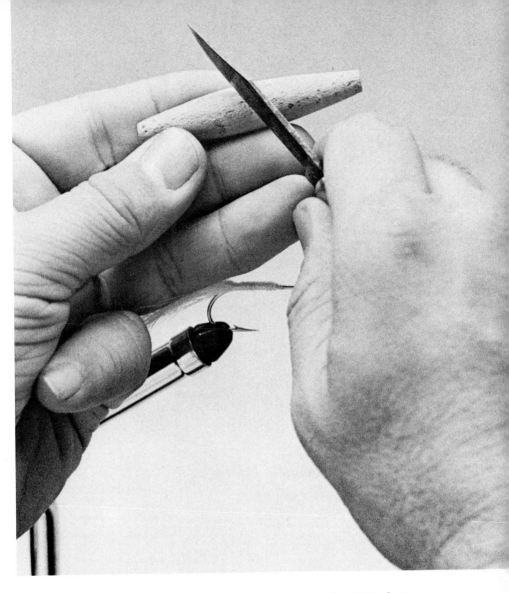

Preparation of the cork body is the next step. Cork in this 2½-inch size and shape is available in tackle stores, sometimes called a "perch float"; from one such piece, bodies for two KaBoomBoom Poppers can be made. Cut the cork float into two equal parts, at a 45-degree angle. Each piece now measures 1⅜ inches on top and 1⅛ inches on the bottom.

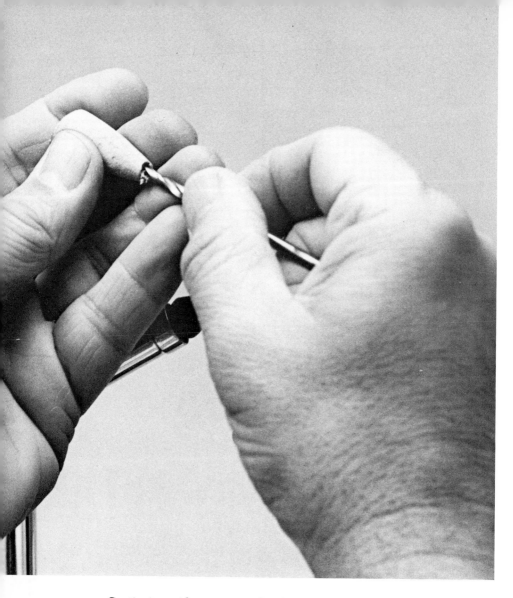

Continuing with one piece of cork, with an electric drill and a ⅛-inch bit remove a little of the cork in the small end. This must be worked carefully, since cork has a tendency to crumble.

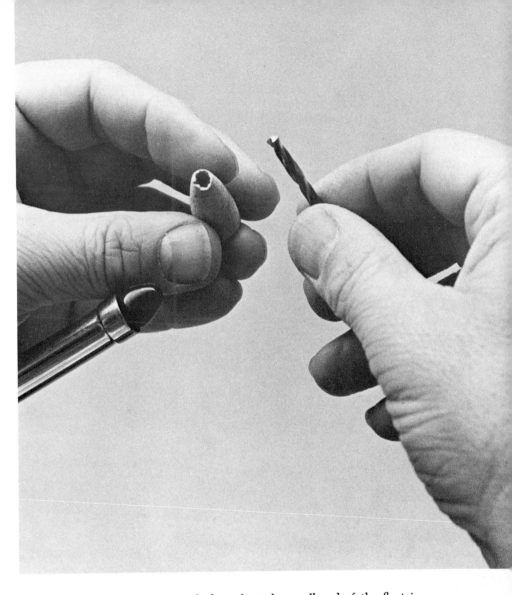

It is necessary to remove a little cork at the small end of the float in order to accommodate a portion of the tail binding.

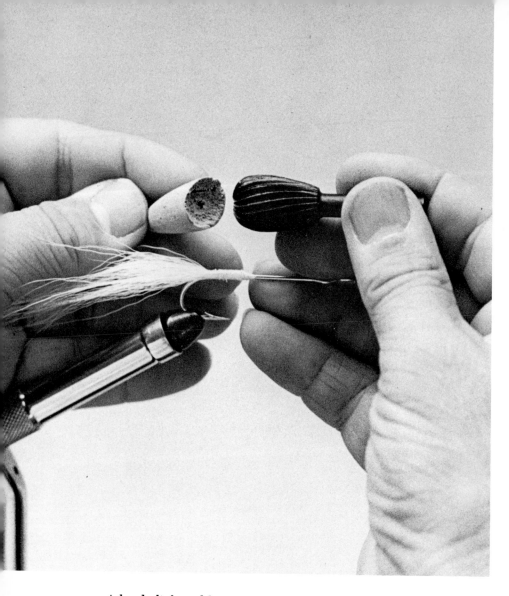

A handy little tool known as a rotary file or ground burr, available at hardware stores, is used to shape the face of the cork body. By touching the cork lightly with it a few times, you can create a shallow concave surface which will become the "popping" front of the body.

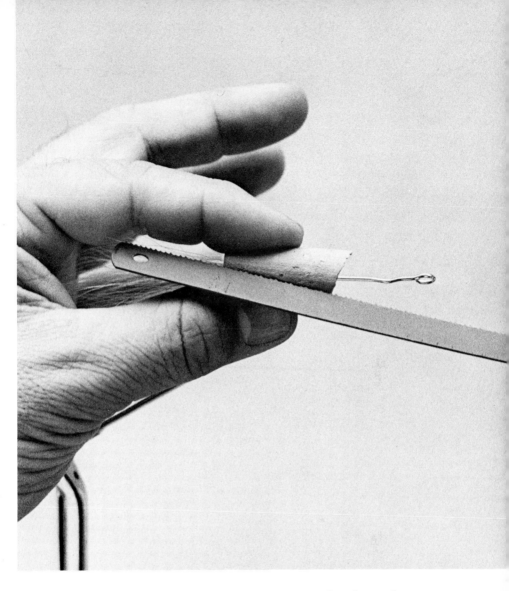

Using a hacksaw or similar thin-bladed saw, make a lengthwise slot in the cork body, just halfway through. Keep the 1⅜-inch measurement of the body uppermost.

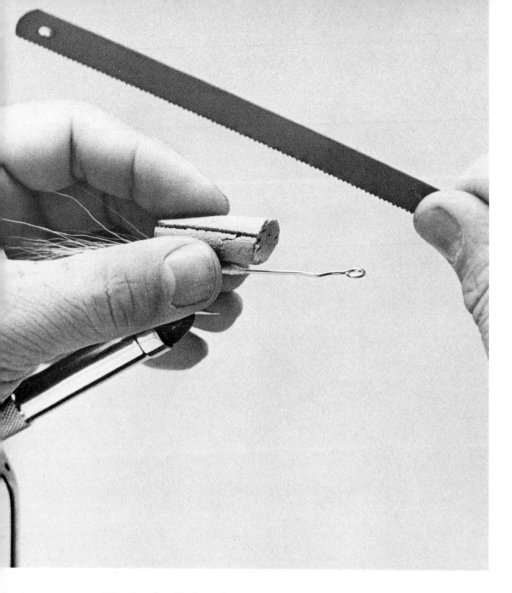

The slot should slant downward a trifle, from center at the small end to a little below center at the wide end.

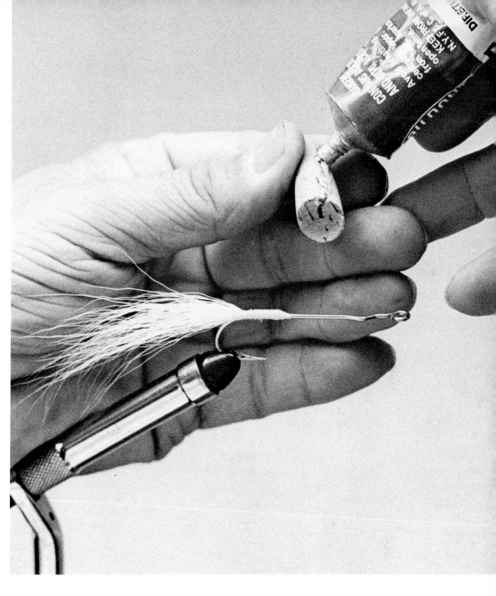

Fill the slot completely with a hard-drying heavy-bodied cement by placing the mouth of the tube against the slot and forcing in the cement.

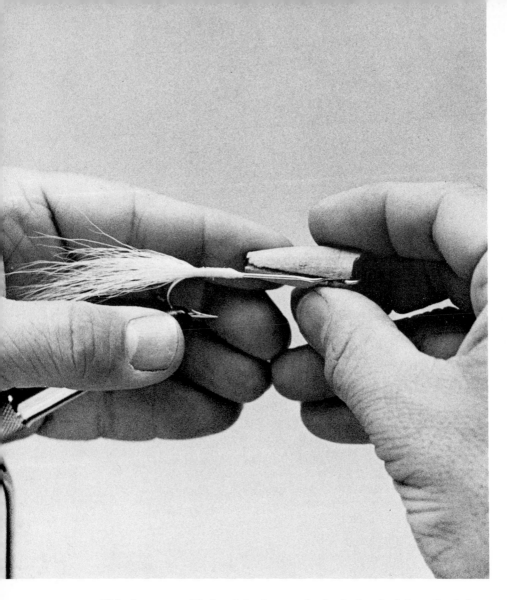

Slide the cement-filled cork body onto the hook ahead of the tail winding and ease it back along the hook until the forward end of the tail winding is covered.

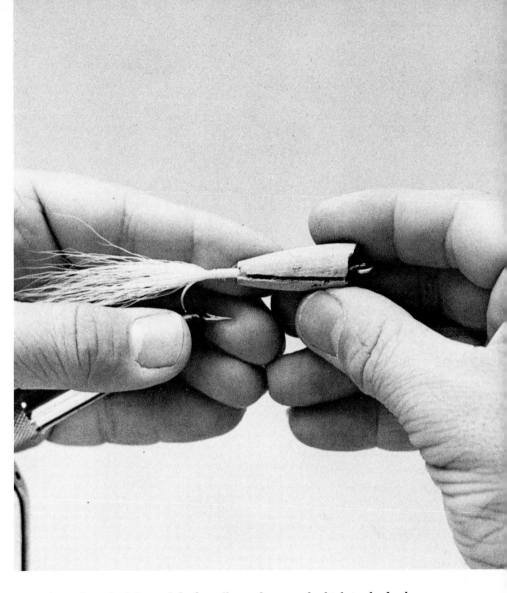

The wide end of the cork body will now be over the kink in the hook. Wipe off any cement that has oozed out of the slot and fill with more, forcing it in again directly from the tube. Allow the cement to set, preferably overnight.

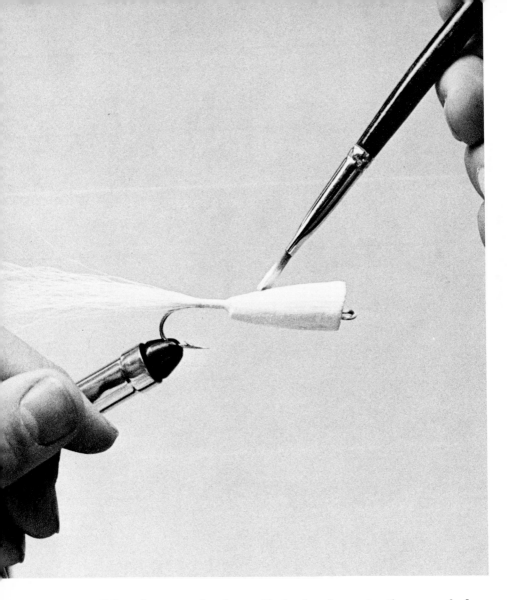

When the cement has thoroughly hardened, examine the popper body for smoothness. Rough edges can be removed carefully with fine sandpaper. Finish by covering the body and tail winding with several coats of quick-drying white lacquer.

The
Shrimp Fly

Any review of the types of salt water patterns in common use today would not be complete without showing the basic shrimp pattern and how it is tied. The procedure shown here is for the grass shrimp, as tied by Louis "Bub" Church, who generously presented us with one of his own tying.

The Shrimp Fly, in a wide range of colors, is used on both coasts by fly rodders and for a variety of game fish. A pink shrimp has been used in San Francisco Bay with great success for striped bass.

It is also a basic fly in Florida on bonefish and, as Joe Brooks points out, it is an important all-around salt water pattern. In one of his letters, he tells that many years ago he had the tyer of a "western shrimp" adapt one to his requirements by making it all pink. It was an immediate success on the bonefish flats, in various sizes depending upon the depth of the water being fished, from a No. 6 hook for eight-inch water to a No. 2 hook for water up to four feet deep.

Paul Kukonen, among many others, has used another adaptation of the shrimp pattern successfully for years in Narragansett Bay, Rhode Island, for weakfish (or squeteague, as they call them).

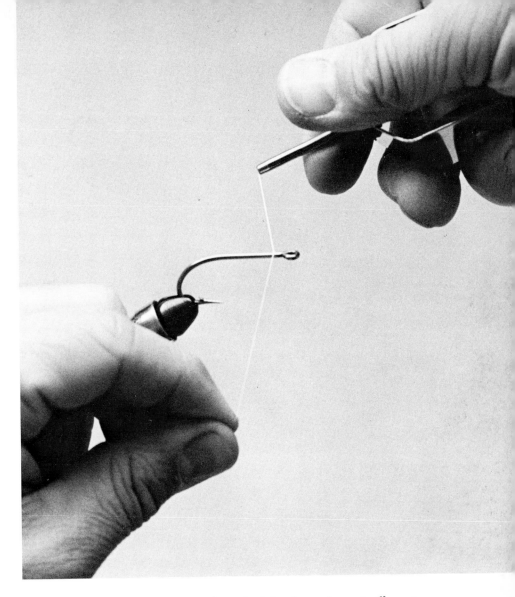

A No. 1/0 regular-length ringed-eye hook has been chosen to illustrate this fly, although it is frequently tied on hooks as small as a No. 2. We have had excellent success with the 1/0 size. Attach the tying thread a short distance behind the hook eye.

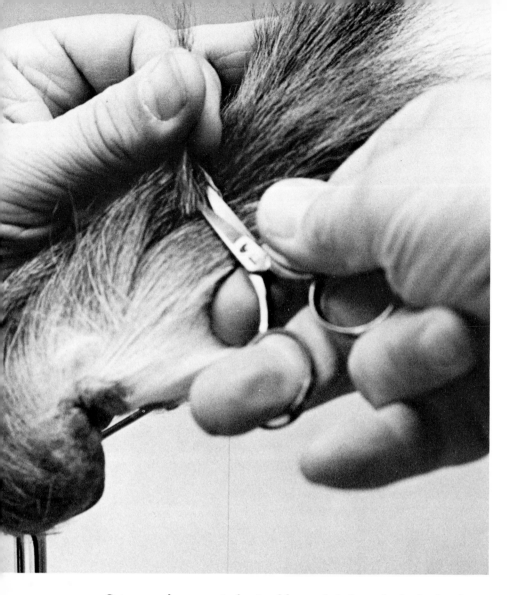

Cut an ample segment of natural brown hair from the back of a deer tail, using the longest hair available, at least 3½ inches in length.

Distribute some lacquer through the cut ends of the hair where it will be bound on the hook, and then tie it on as for a tail. About 1 inch of the hair will be fastened to the hook shank forward of the hook bend. Do not permit the hair to wrap around the hook; keep it all on top.

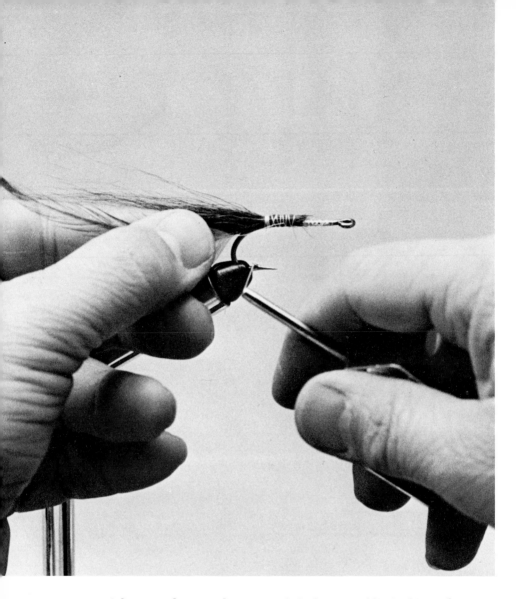

Select a medium-sized ginger or light brown saddle hackle, and tie it in at the base of the tail.

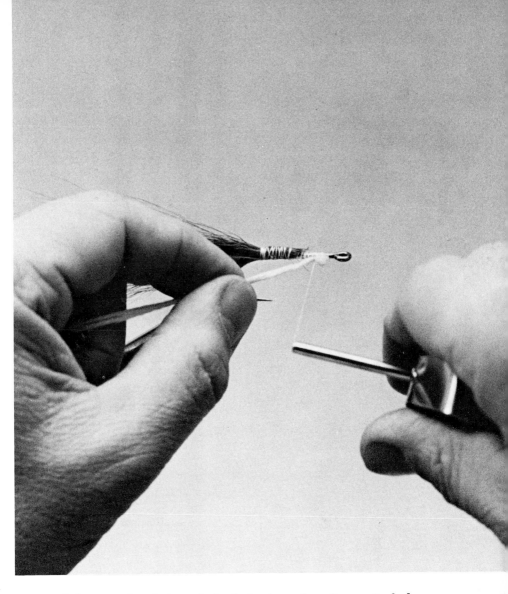

Wind the tying thread along the hook shank to where it was attached, and tie on a double strand of fine-gauge pink nylon yarn, about 12 or 13 inches in length for ease in handling.

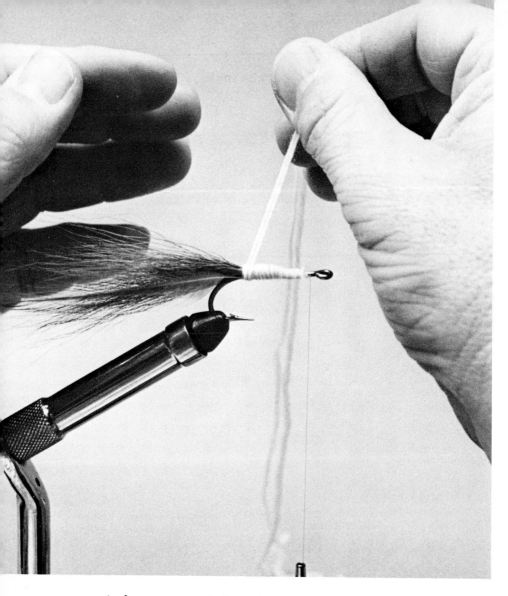

As the yarn covers the base of the hair tail, it will create a body that is uneven in thickness, which is correct. The shrimp body should be contoured in this manner.

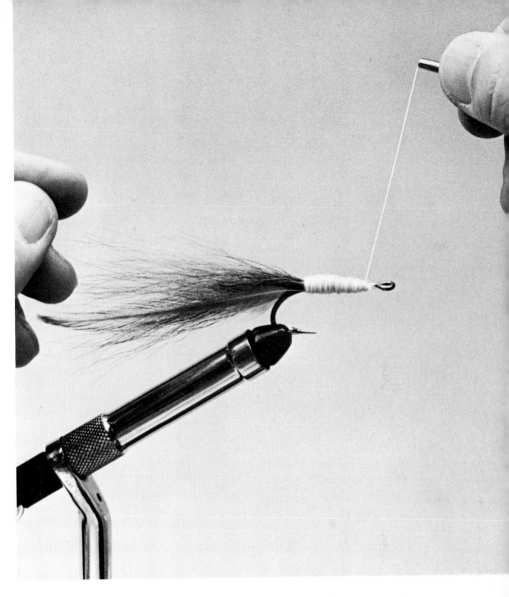

In winding the yarn forward along the hook shank, make sure that the body tapers to about half the size it is at the tail. Cut off the excess yarn.

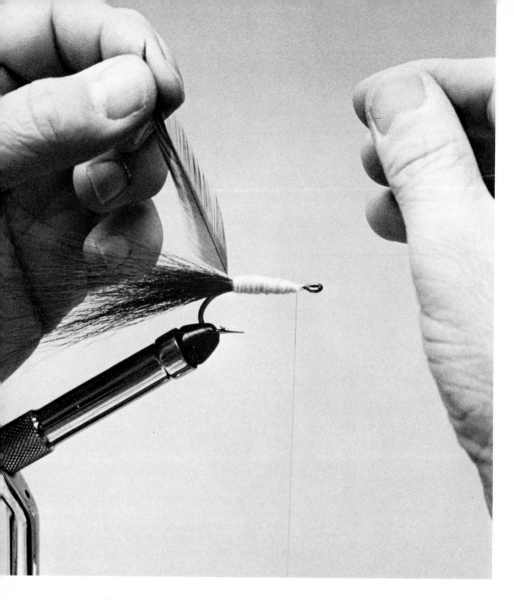

Prepare to wind on the hackle, which will become the legs of the shrimp pattern, so that the natural curve of the feather will be toward the hook eye. It is important to have the shiny (or right) side of the feather toward the tail when the winding begins.

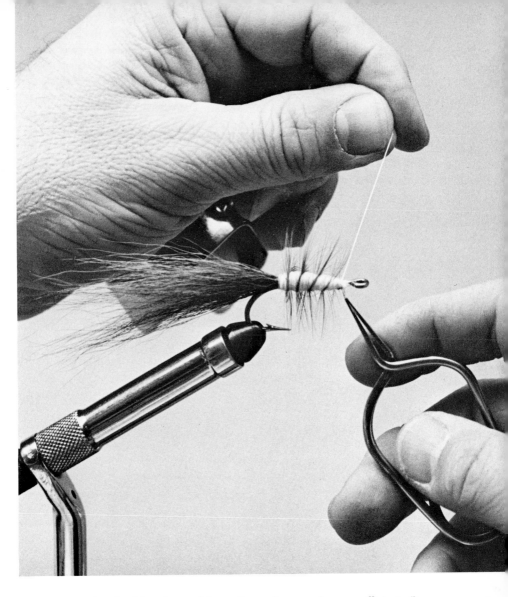

Four or five hackle ribs, widely and evenly spaced, are sufficient. It helps to use hackle pliers to hold the tip of the hackle while it is being caught with the tying thread.

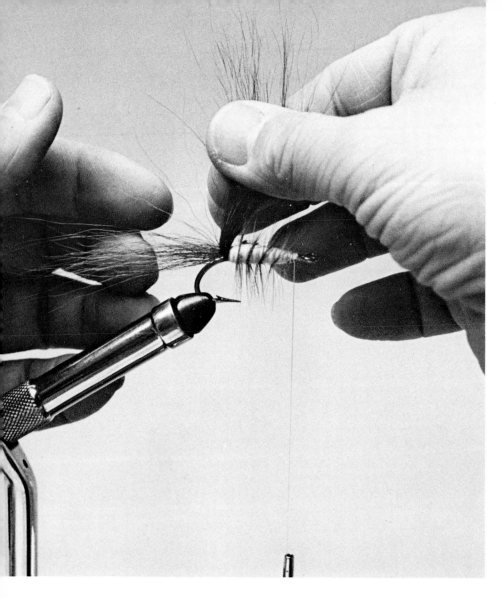

Clip away the hackle barbs directly on top of the body, and separate the upper two thirds of the hair that forms the tail from the rest.

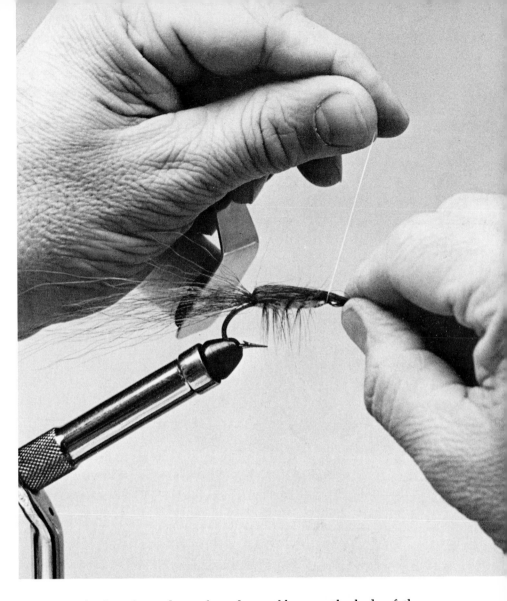

Draw this hair forward, snugly and smoothly, over the body of the shrimp fly, holding it taut while bringing the tying thread up and across it.

Bind it securely to the hook, covering the trimmed ends of the nylon yarn body with the winding at the same time.

Divide the hair that extends beyond the hook eye into two equal parts and separate them by crossing the thread over each in turn. Do not be afraid to pull the hair back and to each side, in order to accomplish the separation.

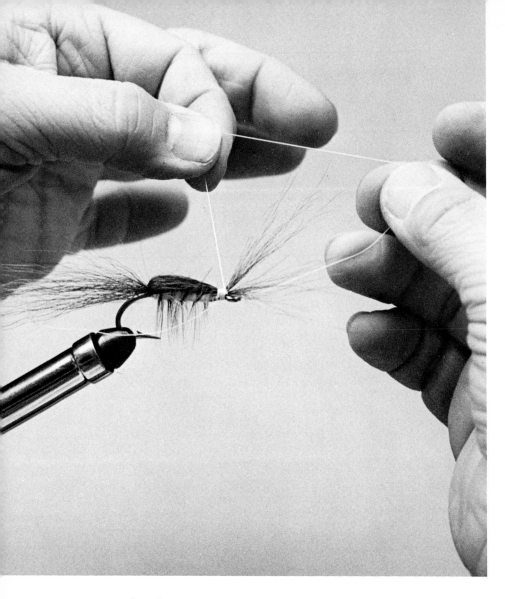

Complete the tying with a whip finish behind the antennae, across the collar, or head.

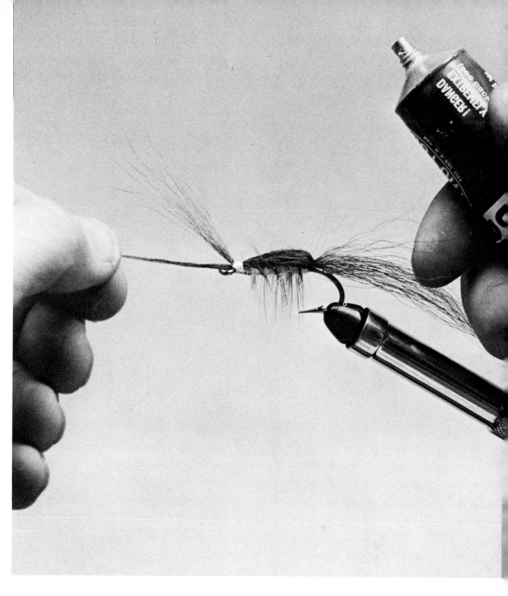

Stiffen the feelers by placing a drop of clear lacquer between thumb and finger and applying to each. When the lacquer is set, trim feelers to about 1 inch in length.

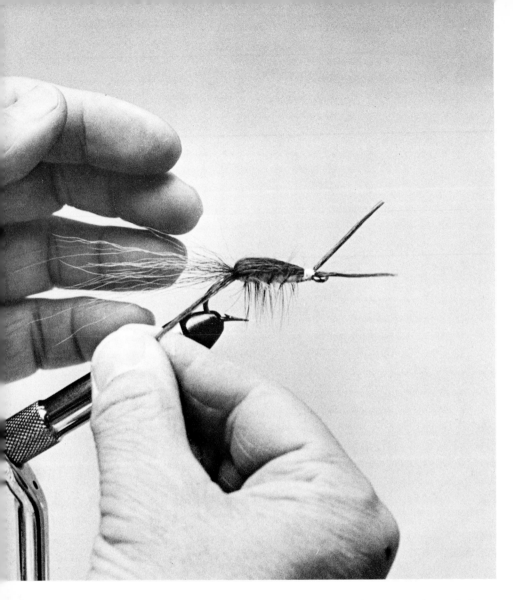

Divide the tail into two equal parts also, and apply a drop of the lacquer between the fingers to them too. When these have hardened, they may be left full length.

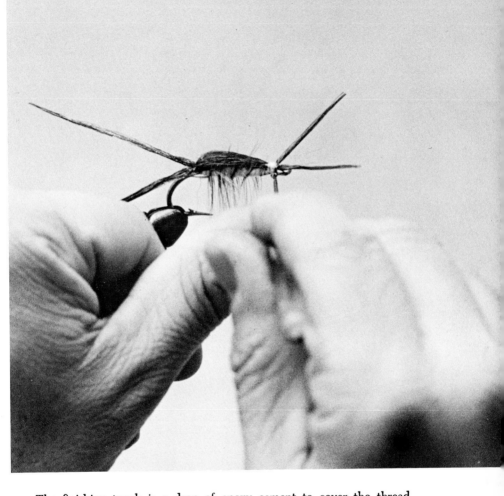

The finishing touch is a drop of epoxy cement to cover the thread collar behind the antennae and the juncture of tails and body.

The Frankee-Belle
Bonefish Fly

Numerous letters from our contributors of flies and anecdotes have
included the Frankee-Belle Bonefish Fly as a must for this book.
In one of his letters, Joe Brooks says, "It was one of the earliest
patterns tied for bonefish and, to my mind, one of the very greatest.
I used it only a month ago, in size No. 4, to take a ten-pound bone
at Key Biscayne."

The fly was named for Frankee Albright and Belle Mathers, and
we are happy to relate that Frankee is still the only woman licensed
to guide fishermen. Her home base is Islamorada, Florida.

Among the sportsmen who have added to the glory of the
Frankee-Belle Bonefish Fly are the renowned dry-fly fresh water
authority, George L. M. La Branche, who fished it in 1947; Bart

Foth; Lefty Kreh; and Lee Cuddy, who has a record catch of 2,000 bonefish for his time at it.

The popular hook sizes are No. 2 and No. 1 down to No. 1/0.

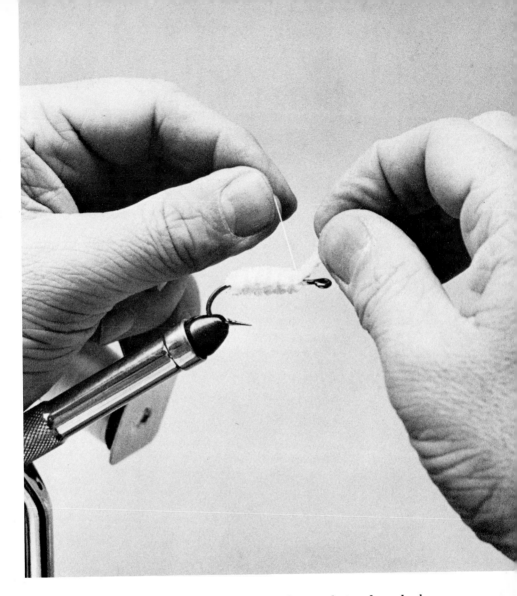

Cover the straight shank of a No. 1/0 stainless steel ringed-eye hook with two layers of white chenille, ending the body about ¼ inch behind the hook eye.

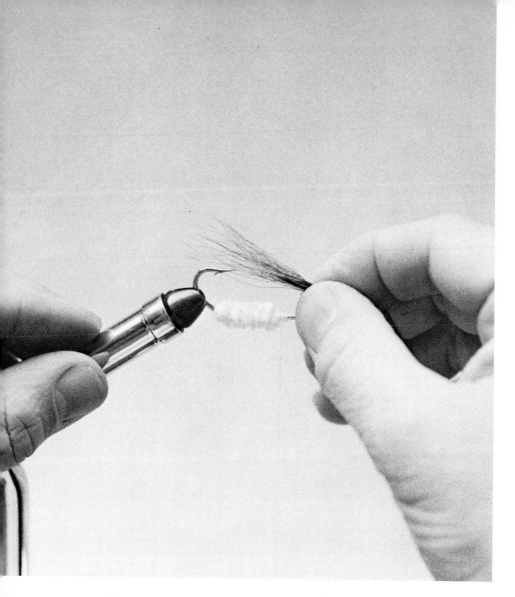

The remaining materials will be tied on the underside of the hook, and some tyers find this easier to accomplish by reversing the hook in the vise, as shown. A small amount of light brown bucktail hair, just long enough to extend about ¾ inch behind the hook, has been clipped from an undyed deer tail. The hair should be taken from an area near the tip of the tail where the hair is fine. (The base of a deer tail may have hair similar in texture to body hair, too coarse for use here.)

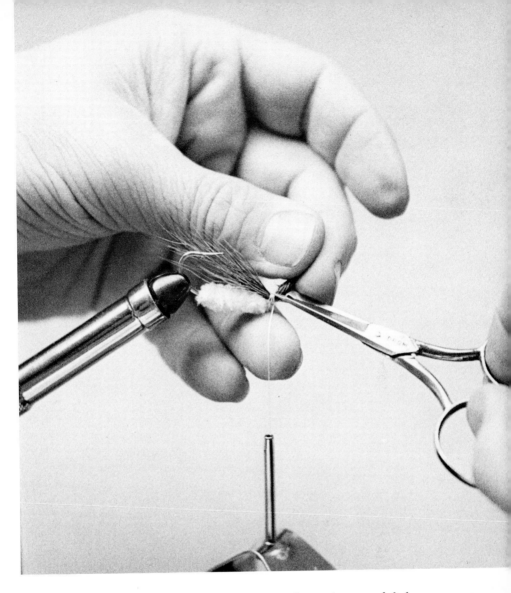

Tie the hair between the hook eye and the body, in the space left for this purpose, and trim away the excess by tapering the stubs to make a neat base for the fly head.

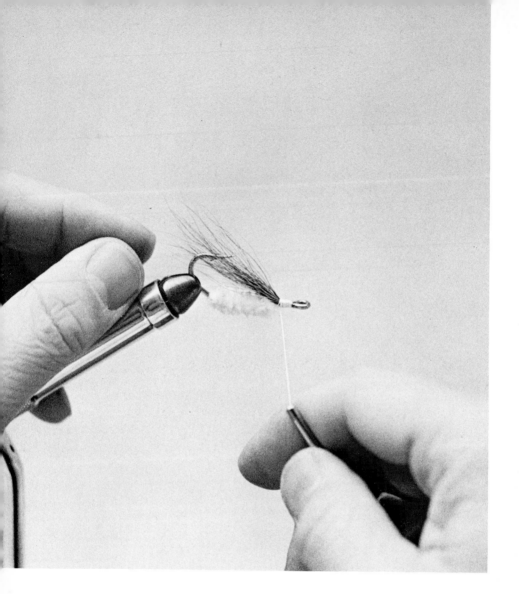

Cover the cut ends of hair, working the tying thread back from the hook eye to the chenille body and covering the cut end of the chenille as well.

Select two slim grizzly hackles from a neck pad. The hackles should be about three quarters of the length of the deer hair, after they have been tied on.

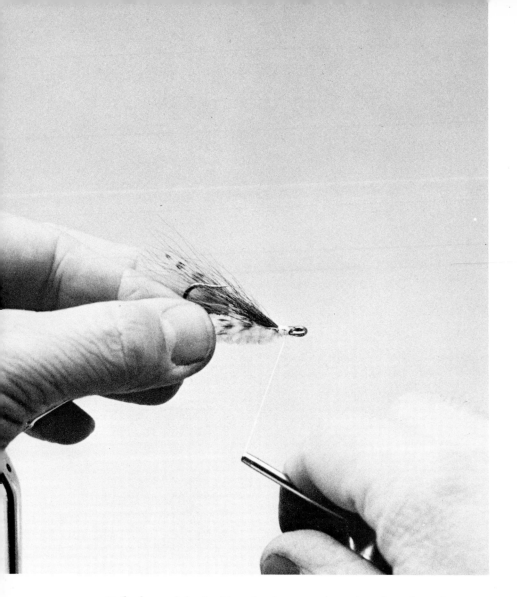

At the base of the hackles, the flues may be stripped or clipped away from the quills before being tied on. (Clipping leaves a rough edge along the quill which helps lock in the feather.) Place one hackle on each side of the head, close to the hair and parallel to it, dull side against the hair.

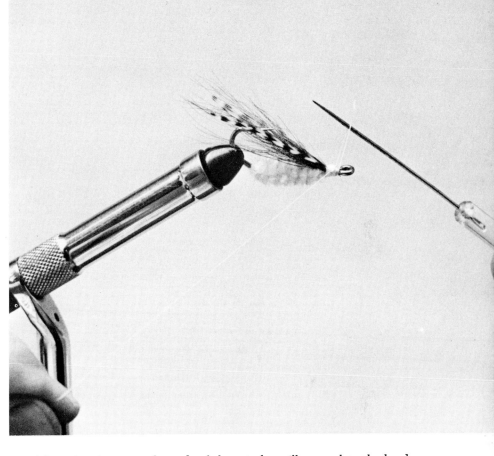

After trimming away the ends of the grizzly quills, complete the head with a whip finish. Many tyers find a needle point useful to hold the loop taut as the thread is pulled through at the finish. A coat or two of lacquer or epoxy cement on the head will protect it.

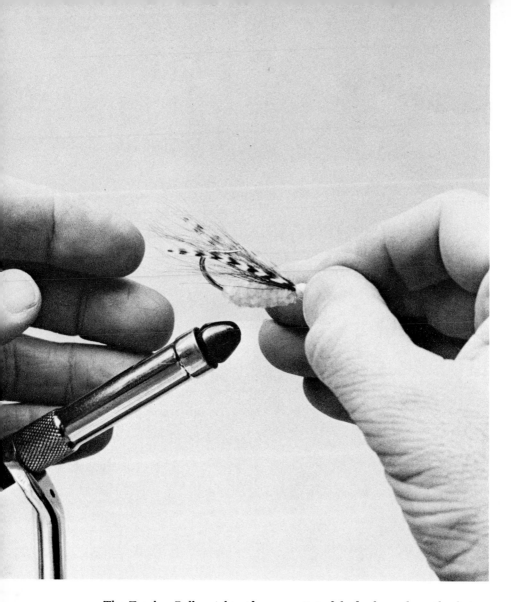

The Frankee-Belle, right side up as it is fished, shows how the hair and hackles cover the point and barb of the hook, making it semi-weedless and furnishing some protection to the sharp point.

The Honey Blonde Keel Fly

The Keel Hook has been chosen to complete the fly-tying sequences of basic salt water patterns. This hook is now readily available in stainless steel and appears to be gaining in appeal among fishermen on both coasts. It is suitable for fly fishing generally and has some advantages in critical areas, which we all run into when fishing.

Its basic design causes it to ride hook up and prevents it from fouling or catching on any bottom debris when used in shallow waters. As you know, many bonefish patterns tied on conventional hooks are tied in reverse, so the hook point rides up; here we have an obvious application.

Any pattern in this book can be tied on a Keel Hook, including the poppers. This should be kept in mind for those times when every retrieve brings back a bundle of weeds that have been floating

115

loose in the ocean. A few of each of your patterns should be made on this hook, and, if made with a reasonably heavy wing, it should contend with any weed condition you may come up against.

Too, in these days of increasing popularity of the sinking fly line, we have a companion hook for this form of fishing.

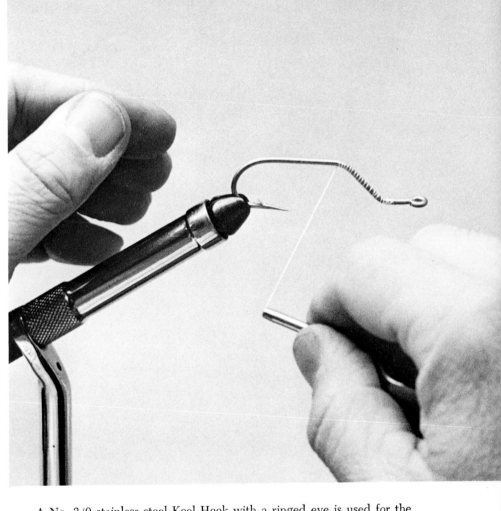

A No. 3/0 stainless steel Keel Hook with a ringed eye is used for the Honey Blonde. Start by attaching the tying thread a short distance behind the hook eye, and wind it the entire length of the shank, stopping just above the barb.

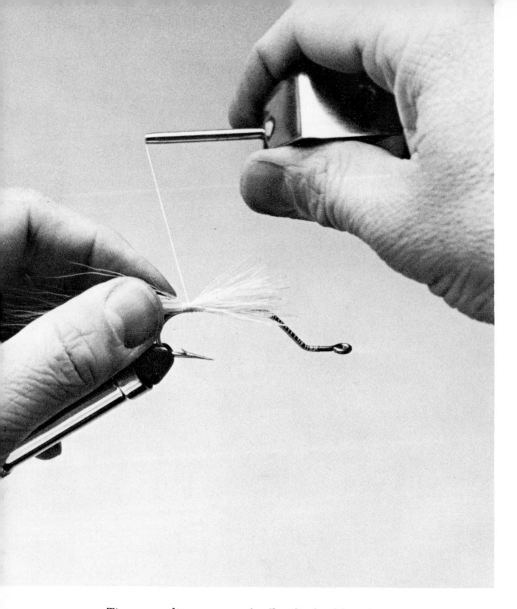

Tie on a medium amount of yellow bucktail hair, long enough to cover the straight shank of the hook and extend 2 inches beyond the end, above the barb, with the cut ends covering the hook shank on top.

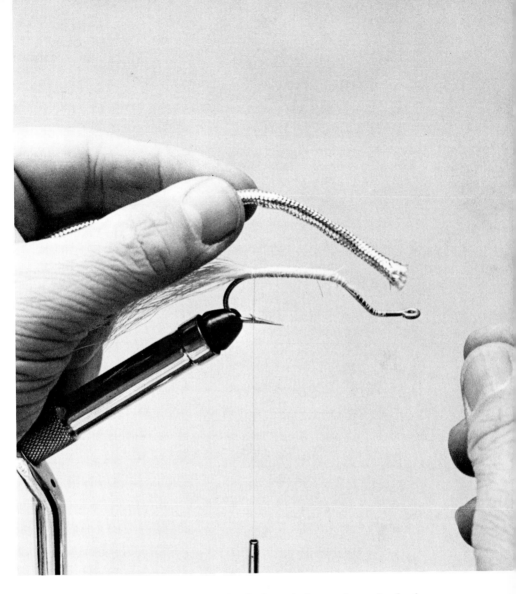

The yellow deer hair has been firmly bound down along the hook shank and the tying thread wound back to the base of the tail. Measure a piece of Mylar tubing, or piping, against the Keel Hook, for the approximate length to use, and cut off a trifle more to allow for ease in handling it.

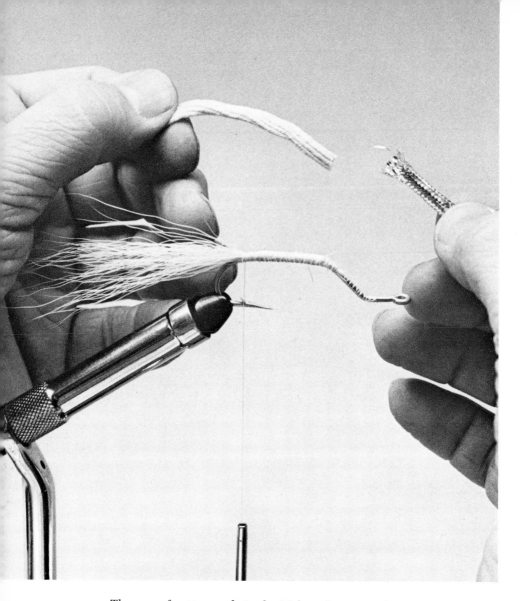

The core of cotton cords in the Mylar tubing must be removed before the tube can be slipped onto the hook. Be careful to fray as few of the Mylar strands as possible.

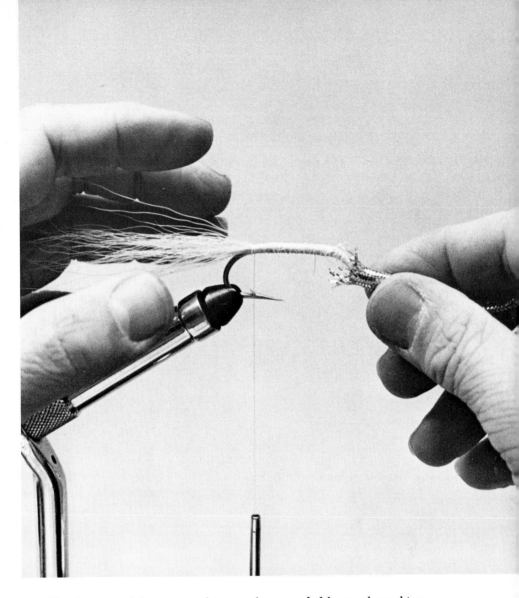

The diameter of the woven tubing can be expanded by gently pushing the ends toward each other, or it can be decreased by pulling them. Here the tubing has been expanded in order to slip it easily over the hook eye and onto the hook.

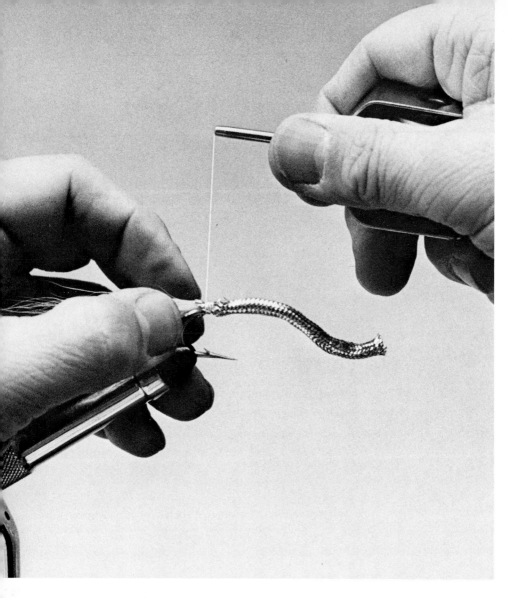

Ease the Mylar tubing all the way back to the tail, and gently bring the tying thread through the unraveled end, allowing the ends of the Mylar strands to extend beyond. (They will be removed later.) Bind down the tubing and whip-finish this end above the barb.

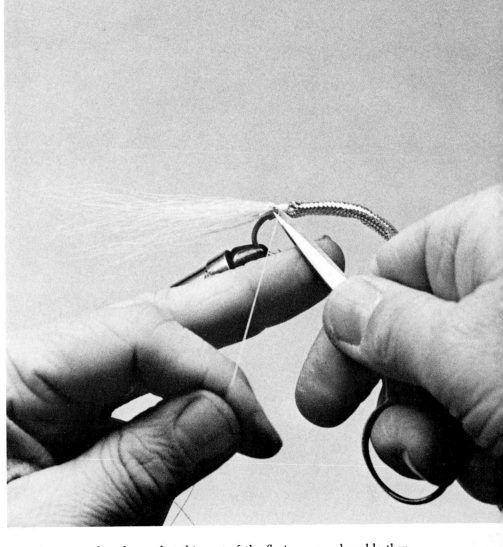

Experience has shown that this part of the fly is more vulnerable than any other, so make sure all of the strands of Mylar have been covered with the whip finish before clipping off the thread and trimming away the protruding strands of Mylar, as close to the winding as possible.

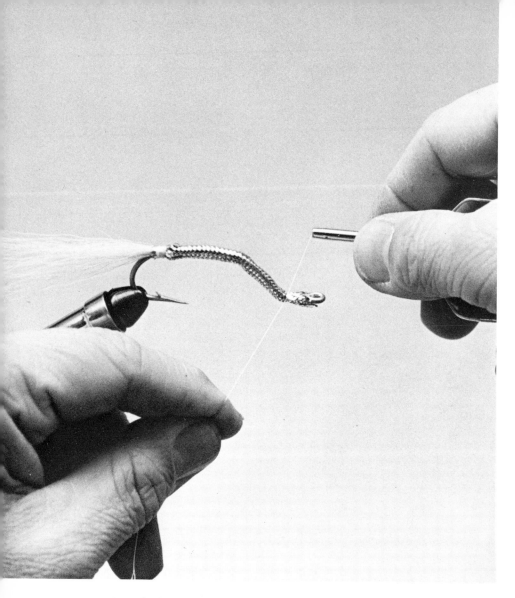

Smooth the Mylar tubing forward along the hook toward the eye, decreasing its diameter and working out any buckling that may occur. Attach the tying thread again, over the Mylar, just ahead of the bend, near the eye. Wind the tying thread over the Mylar, to cover the first bend in the hook, and back again to the short, straight part behind the eye. Clip off the exposed Mylar strands.

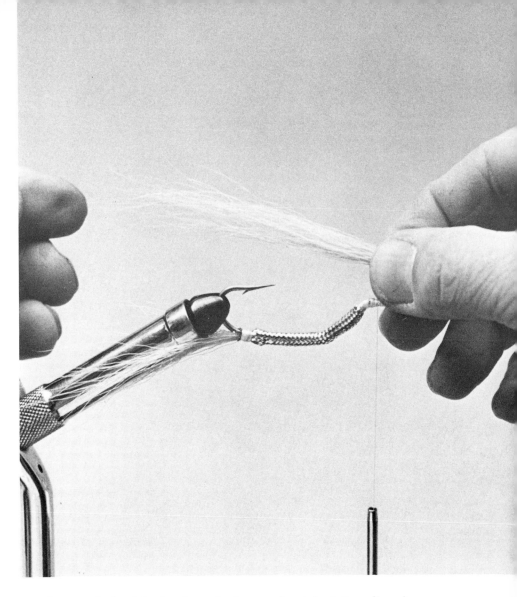

Reverse the hook in the vise and select another tuft of the yellow deer hair, in an amount equal to that of the tail and long enough to extend about 1 inch beyond the hook. Tie this wing securely on the short, straight portion of the hook behind the hook eye.

The wing of the Honey Blonde will extend straight back from the eye, over the point and barb. This fly is right side up when upside down, a characteristic of the Keel Hook. Coat the whip-finished head with several applications of clear lacquer, carefully including the winding that covers the hook bend, beneath the wing.

Fifty Popular Patterns

For practical purposes we have had to reduce the number of flies presented to us, but following are representatives of all the popular patterns submitted by seasoned salt water fly fishermen. Some may be traced back to the beginning of this century, while others are as recent as 1950. Some patterns have been used with equal success on the West Coast as well as in North Atlantic and Florida waters. In many cases several salt water species have succumbed to the lure of one specific fly.

Therefore it seemed simpler to organize the flies according to construction—streamers, shrimp types, floaters and poppers, and others—rather than variety of fish.

The photograph of each fly is accompanied by the pattern and the name of its contributor.

White Whistler Red
(*Striped bass*)

Hook: Nos. 1/0–5/0, short shank
Tail: Heavy white bucktail 3½ inches long
Body: Weighted with lead wire and covered
  with red chenille
Hackle: Three long webby saddle hackles dyed
  bright red, thickly palmered
Eyes: Two medium chain beads
Head: Red thread
Note: Colors may be reversed or a combination
  of yellow and orange used
Dan Blanton, San Jose, California

Bay Dredger
(*Striped bass*)

Hook: Nos. 2/0–3/0
Body: Gold Mylar tubing wrapped over
  weighted and padded body
Wing: Thick bucktail, white next to body with
  blue and green over, in that order; twelve
  strands of peacock herl over all
Head: Large and white, ½ inch long
Throat: Painted red stripes under head
Eyes: Medium bead chain eyes
Bob Edgley and Dan Blanton, San Jose, California

Rhody Three-Wing: Gibbs Special
(*Striped bass and bluefish*)

Hook: No. 4, streamer
Tail: Yellow bucktail, 1 inch long
Body: Silver chenille
Wing: Length, to bend of hook; blue bucktail
  over yellow, in middle of back, yellow buck-
  tail at head
Beards: Yellow bucktail in middle of body, red
  bucktail at head
Cheeks: Jungle cock breast feather
Al Brewster, Riverside, Rhode Island

Argentine Blonde
(*Various species*)

Hook: Nos. 1/0–3/0
Tail: White bucktail
Body: Silver tinsel
Wings: Blue bucktail
Other blondes:
    Strawberry (orange/red)
    Platinum (white/white)
    Honey (yellow/yellow)
    Black with black
    Pink with pink
Originated by Joe Brooks

Seminarian
(*Bluefish*)

Hook: No. 3/0, 5XL shank
Tail: Yellow impala
Body: Six evenly spaced bunches of yellow
    impala, top and bottom of hook shank; rear
    three wrapped with 20-pound dark green
    monofilament, remainder with dark red
Head: Black
Tom Camara, Warwick, Rhode Island

No Name
(*Striped bass, bluefish, and weakfish*)

Hook: Nos. 1/0–3/0, XL shank
Body: None
Wings: White nylon hair, from 2 to 4 inches
    long
Shoulder (optional): Mallard breast feather
Herb Chase, Portsmouth, Rhode Island

129

Bub's Red Herring
(*Striped bass*)

Hook: No. 1/0
Body: Silver Mylar tubing, 3½ inches long, tied behind hook eye and allowed to trail
Wings: White nylon crimped hair next to body, straight nylon hair in orange and blue, over in that order, as long as body; peacock herl over all
Throat: White bucktail to end of body
Head: Large and red, coated with epoxy
Eye: Yellow with black center
Bub Church, Plainfield, New Jersey

Bub's Tinker Mackerel
(*Striped bass*)

Hook: No. 1/0
Body: None
Wings: White bucktail 3½ inches long; green dyed grizzly hackle feather on each side, four 1/64-inch Mylar strips on each side; peacock herl over all
Throat: Two white saddle hackles 3½ inches long
Cheek: Dark green pheasant with yellow painted eye
Head: Black, epoxy coated
Bub Church, Plainfield, New Jersey

Spiro
(*Striped bass, bluefish, weakfish, tarpon, and snook*)

Hook: No. 3/0, keel type
Tail: White bucktail, sparse, with three white saddle hackles over
Body: Gold Mylar tubing with red fluorescent rib
Wing: White bucktail next to body, red bucktail next, then white bucktail mixed with six strands of 1/64-inch gold Mylar; wing extending beyond hook bend; each segment of hair rather sparse
Throat: Short red calf hair
Collar: Red hackle
Cap Colvin, Jensen Beach, Florida

Orange Blossom Marabou
(*Striped bass and other species*)

Hook: No. 2/0
Tail: 4-inch marabou feathers dyed bright red-
orange
Body: Orange chenille (or black)
Head: Black
Other "Blossoms":
Apple (white/white)
Cherry (pink/pink)
Lemon (yellow/yellow)
Plum (blue/blue)
Blackberry (black/black)
George Cornish, Avalon, New Jersey
Credit: Cornish, Sosin, Wood

No Name
(*Hickory shad and sea robin*)

Hook: No. 4
Tail: Golden pheasant tippet
Body: Orange seal fur
Rib: Silver tinsel halfway
Hackle: Yellow tied palmer, clipped to taper
toward tail
Wing case: Nymph-style light blue saddle
hackle fibers
Armand Courchaine, Somerset, Massachusetts

Freddie Green
(*Striped bass, albacore, yellowtail*)

Hook: No. 5/0
Tail: White bucktail 3½ inches long, 1/64-inch
silver Mylar strip at each side, green bucktail
3 inches long tied between tail and body
Body: Silver Mylar tinsel
Wings: White bucktail 3½ inches long next to
body, green bucktail 2½ inches long over;
one strip 1/64-inch silver Mylar on each side;
twelve strands peacock herl over all
Head: Black
Eye: Yellow with red center
Dave Cox, Altadena, California
(Courtesy of Freddie, his wife)

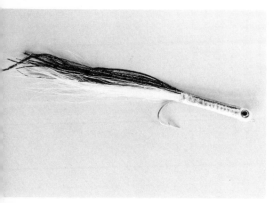

D'Allesandro Balsa Streamer
(*Striped bass*)

Hook: No. 5/0, XL shank
Body: Oval balsa wood, white bucktail hair 5
    inches long covering; twelve strands of pea-
    cock herl to end of hair, forming tail (on
    top of back); strip of metallic silver contact
    tape on each side of body; entire body
    wrapped with clear PVC (polyvinyl chloride)
    and sealed with clear vinyl cement
Head: White
Eye: Red glass, 4 mm
John D'Allesandro, Bridgeport, Connecticut

Gary Dyer Pattern No. 1
(*Striped bass*)

Hook: Nos. 4/0–6/0
Tail: Bucktail 3 inches long, white over red
    over chartreuse
Body: Silver Mylar piping, wrapped
Wing: 3½-inch bucktail, heavy; white next to
    body, chartreuse and blue over, in that order
Head: Black
Eye: Yellow
Gary Dyer, Coos Bay, Oregon

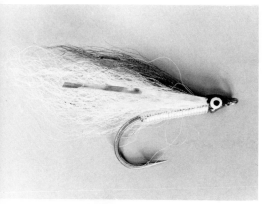

Glass Minnow (Sea Flies Series)
(*Bonito, mackerel, snapper, bluefish*)

Hook: No. 1/0
Body: Clear monofilament over silver Mylar
    base
Wing: Green bucktail over white
Cheek: 1/32-inch silver Mylar strip on each
    side, three fourths of wing
Chico Fernandez, Miami, Florida

Beer Belly Streamer
(*Striped bass*)

Hook: No. 6/0
Tail: Bucktail, green over yellow, 1½ inches long
Body: Silver Mylar tubing over tear-shaped aluminum piece folded over hook and crimped in place, filled with epoxy
Wings: Green over orange bucktail, 3½ inches long
Larry Green, San Bruno, California

No Name
(*Striped bass*)

Hook: No. 5/0 (various sizes optional)
Tail: Bucktail, purple over white
Body: Blue and white hackle, mixed, tied palmer over black thread base
Head: Black
Myron Gregory, Oakland, California

Ugly Duckling
(*Bluefish*)

Hook: 2 to 3 inches long
Body: None
Wing: Hackle feathers tied flat on top and trailing 1 inch beyond hook, brown over blue over red over white
Head: Long, red, tapered to hook eye
George Heinhold. Madison, Connecticut
Adapted by Paul Hiller and Peter Klinkowski of Norwalk, Connecticut

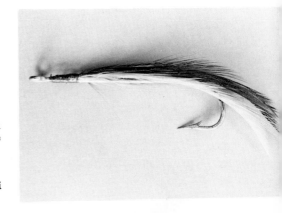

Janssen Bullhead
(*Striped bass*)

Hook: No. 4/0
Body: Gold tinsel
Underwing: Fox squirrel
Centerwing: Molted ostrich feather (or very light grizzly hackle)
Overwing: Four cree hackles with two hen pheasant body feathers over, all tied flat on top
Cheeks: Hen pheasant body feathers curving away from body with tips forward
Head: Varied shades of natural brown deer hair, spun and clipped
Hal Janssen, Lafayette, California

Janssen Striper Fly

Hook: No. 3/0
Body: Silver Mylar tinsel
Wing: Bucktail, pale green over blue, 2½ inches long
Throat: White bucktail, same length; note that wing and throat veil body
Head: Colors of bucktail extended onto head with matching paint
Eye: Yellow with black center
Note: Wing colors and hook sizes may be varied
Hal Janssen, Layfayette, California

Cockroach
(*Tarpon*)

Hook: No. 1/0 stainless steel, ringed eye
Body: None
Tail: Two pairs of grizzly hackles 2½ inches long
Wing: Natural brown bucktail, tied completely around hook and flowing back as a collar, sparse
Lefty Kreh, Miami, Florida

134

Eight Featured Flies

The Platinum Blonde

Lefty's Deceiver

The Blockbuster

The Tarpon Fly

The KaBoomBoom Popper

The Shrimp Fly

The Frankee-Belle Bonefish Fly

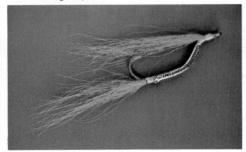

The Honey Blonde Keel Fly

Nine Classics

From our correspondence and the records reviewed, the following nine patterns may be deemed old enough and sufficiently alluring to game fish of the brine to have earned their places as classics.

Bonbright Tarpon Fly

Hook: No. 5/0
Tail: Red and white hackle tips, 1 inch long
Body: Silver tinsel
Wings: White saddle hackles 2½ inches long
Cheeks: Red swan and jungle cock eye
Hackle: White
Originator: Howard Bonbright

Dean Bead Head
(*Small tarpon, bonefish, ladyfish*)

Hook: No. 1/0
Body: Yellow chenille
Wings: Four white neck hackles, 2½ inches long, each pair flared outward
Collar: Dark grizzly or grizzly and black mixed
Head: Lightweight wooden bead painted yellow
Eye: Black with red center
Originator: Gordon Dean
This original, tied in early 1950s, was lent by Gordon Dean, New York, New York

Palmer Diller
(*Striped bass*)

Hook: No. 1/0
Body: Silver tinsel
Wings: Bucktail, blue next to body, red next, and white over in equal amounts
Originator: Harvey Flint

Gibbs Striper Fly

Hook: No. 1/0
Body: Silver tinsel
Wings: White bucktail
Throat: Dyed red hackle fibers
  ¼ inch in length
Cheek: Jungle cock breast
  feathers over blue swan
Originator: Harold Gibbs
This original, tied by Harold
  Gibbs in March, 1950, was
  lent by Robert F. Morse of
  Branford, Connecticut.

Loving Bass Fly
(*Striped bass*)

Hook: No. 1/0
Body: None
Wings: White bucktail
Hackle: Dyed red saddle
  hackle
Originator: Tom Loving
This fly, the first known to be
  designed for striped bass, was
  used in Chesapeake Bay in
  the 1920s, according to Joe
  Brooks.

Pigtails

(*Striped bass*)
Hook: No. 1/0
Body: Silver tinsel
Wings: Bucktail—green next to
  body, yellow next, and white
  over; peacock herl over all
Throat: Dyed red hackle fibers
Cheek (optional): Teal
Originator: Edward A. Materne

Horror
(Bonefish and permit)

Hook: Nos. 1/0–3/0
Body: Rear two thirds, yellow chenille ending in narrow band of red thread
Wing: Brown bucktail as a throat 2 inches long beneath hook
Body: Forward third, yellow chenille
Head: Red thread
Originator: P. Perinchief

Rhode Tarpon Streamer

Hook: Nos. 3/0–5/0
Body: Orange hackle-tied palmer three fourths of hook shank, one fourth red thread
Tail: Six to ten white saddle hackles 3 to 5 inches long
Originator: Homer Rhode, Jr.

Sands Bonefish Fly

Hook: No. 1/0
Wing: White bucktail 2 inches long
Cheek: Grizzly hackle over yellow hackle, high on each side
Head: Black
Originator: Hagen Sands

Ballyhoo
(*Various Florida species*)

Hook: No. 1/0
Tail: Twelve white saddle hackles 4 inches long with two 1/32-inch Mylar strips on each side
Body: Built up with tying thread, painted green on top and white underneath
Lefty Kreh, Miami, Florida

Frank Streamer
(*Striped bass*)

Hook: No. 2/0
Tail: Frosty squirrel extending from body tubing
Body: Silver Mylar tubing 1 inch longer than hook
Wings: Purple over white bucktail with heavy peacock herl topping, 3 inches long
Shoulders: Jungle cock eye feathers
Throat: Red hackle fibers
Head: Black
Frank Lawrence, El Sobrante, California

No Name
(*Striped bass*)

Hook: No. 3/0, short shank
Body: Silver Mylar tubing, wrapped
Wings: Yellow over white bucktail in equal amounts, with peacock herl overlay
Cheek: Jungle cock breast feather
Throat: Peacock sword
Eye: White with red center
Howard Laws, Fall River, Massachusetts

Galli-Nipper
(*Striped bass*)

Hook: No. 1/0, 3XL shank
Tail: Red wool ¼ inch long
Body: Silver Mylar piping, wrapped
Wings: Yellow bucktail, 3½ inches long
Cheeks: 2½-inch-long grizzly hackles, placed
high on each side
Throat: Red wool ¼ inch long
Head: Gold
J. Edson Leonard, Barrington, Rhode Island

Lyman's Terror
(*Striped bass*)

Hook: No. 2/0
Body: Silver tinsel
Wings: White over red over white bucktail,
approximately 3 inches long
Cheek: Jungle cock breast feather
Variation: Green in wing instead of red
Originated by Hal Lyman, Boston, Massachu-
setts

McNally Smelt
(*Various species*)

Hook: No. 3/0
Body: Silver Mylar tinsel
Wings: Heavy, of white bucktail 4½ to 5 inches
long; fifteen to twenty peacock herl strands
of same length over
Cheek (optional): Mallard breast feather
Tom McNally, Chicago, Illinois

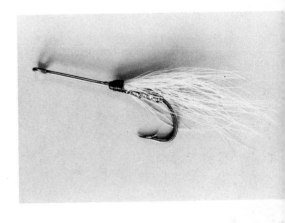

Bluefish Streamer

Hook: No. 2/0, 4XL (or various sizes)
Body: Rear quarter wrapped with fine-diameter
red Mylar piping
Wing: Yellow bucktail 1 inch long, just ahead
of short body
C. Boyd Pfeiffer, Baltimore, Maryland

Simple One
(*Striped bass, bluefish, sea trout*)

Hook: Nos. 6 through 3/0
Body: Silver Mylar (gold for sea trout)
Wings: White bucktail tied completely around
hook (yellow bucktail for sea trout, light
blue for sea bass)
C. Boyd Pfeiffer, Baltimore, Maryland

No-Name Bucktail
(*Bonito*)

Hook: No. 2
Body: Heavy oval silver tinsel
Wing: Layers of dyed bucktail—light yellow
next to body, light green, white, and purple,
in that order, all 3 inches long; strands of
peacock herl half the length of the wing
over all
Head: Black
Eye: White with black center
Allan Rohrer, Long Beach, California

137

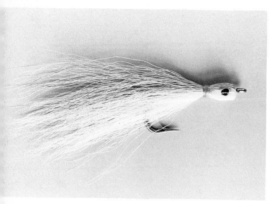

Menhaden Streamer
(*Striped bass and bluefish*)

Hook: Nos. 1/0–3/0
Body: None
Wings: Bucktail, 3½ inches long, white underneath, pink above hook, blue on top; all tied
forward and then back around hook and
secured with a red collar of thread ½ inch
behind hook eye
Eye: Painted orange with black center on pink
stripe between collar and hook eye
Morton Ross, Massapequa Park, New York

Tube Flies
(Not made directly on hook, but adaptable to
any pattern)

Body: Base of plastic bar straw with Mylar
piping over; diameter of straw should be
large enough to accommodate eye of hook
Wings: Colored or white, bucktail or marabou,
tied completely around tube with strips of
1/64-inch Mylar tied in
Note: Tube is threaded on leader before hook
is tied on tippet. Fly will usually slide back
away from hook when fish is caught. Popular
in British Isles for fresh water fishing.
Phil Rush, Old Westbury, New York

Mai Tai
(*Striped bass*)

Hook: No. 1/0
Tail: Unraveled ends of body tubing
Body: Gold or silver Mylar tubing
Wing: Crinkle saran hair—with gold body, yel-
low with orange and black over, in that
order, 2¼ to 3¾ inches long; with silver body,
green in place of orange
Head: Black
Eye: White (on gold body), yellow (on silver
body), with red and black centers on both
Fred Schrier, Toms River, New Jersey

138

No-Name Streamer
(*Tuna and various species*)

Hook: No. 3/0
Body: Silver tinsel
Wings: Intensely blue nylon hair, 3½ inches
    long and rather heavy
Head: Black
Steve Sloan, New York, New York

Solomon Bonefish

Hook: No. 1
Body: None, but strands of silver Mylar at-
    tached ¼ inch behind head
Wing: White bucktail beneath hook, pale olive
    or gray bucktail on top, both tied forward
    over hook eye and then back to surround
    hook completely
Collar: Narrow, red, approximately ⅜ inch be-
    hind hook eye
Eye: Tiny, yellow with black center
Larry Solomon, New York, New York

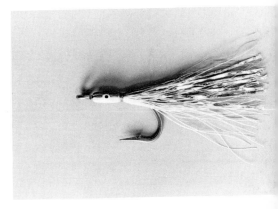

Silver Outcast
(*Various species*)

Hook: No. 4/0
Body: Short, of silver tinsel
Wings: Bucktail, white, 3¼ inches long, com-
    pletely around hook, with smaller amounts of
    yellow and light purple over in that order;
    strands of peacock herl over all
Cheek: Jungle cock eye
Head: Black, about ⅜ inch in length
Originator: Dr. Ralph Daugherty, McKeesport,
    Pennsylvania
Charles F. Waterman, Deland, Florida

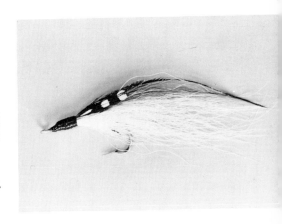

Boyle Shrimp
(*Striped bass*)

Hook: No. 1, bent to have hump
Tail: None
Body: Red fluorescent underbody covered with
   monofilament and lacquered
Rib: Silver tinsel on rear half
Legs: Stiff white pig bristles
Eyes: Small butt ends of white feather quills
   with black lacquered tips
Antennae: ½-inch pig bristles
Robert Boyle, Croton-on-Hudson, New York

Pink Shrimp
(*Bonefish and permit*)

Hook: Nos. 6–2
Tail: Pink bucktail, 1 inch long
Body: Silver tinsel
Hood: Pink bucktail
Hackle: Pink, tied palmer and clipped for legs
Joe Brooks' adaptation of Phillips' Western
   Shrimp

Floating Shrimp
(*Striped bass*)

Hook: No. 2
Tail: Brown bucktail 1 inch long
Body: Clipped deer body hair
Hood: Brown bucktail
Throat: Deer body hair ½ inch long
Tom Camara, Warwick, Rhode Island

140

Grass Shrimp
(*Striped bass*)

Hook: Nos. 2–4
Tail: Two peccary bristles
Body: Light dirty-gray wool dubbing
Rib: Oval silver tinsel and brown thread (No. 0) on forward two thirds of body
Legs: Grizzly hackle palmered and clipped to ½ inch on forward two thirds of body
Hood: Natural brown bucktail
Antennae: Grizzly hackle fibers and bucktail mixed
Eye: Painted black on rear third of body
John Lane, New York, New York

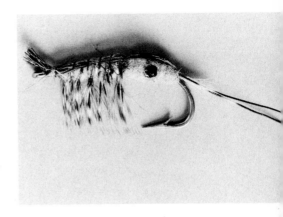

Kukonen Grass Shrimp
(*Sea trout and striped bass*)

Hook: No. 1/0, bent to have hump
Tail: Light brown hackle tips
Body: Padded and wrapped in brown chenille
Hackle: Large and brown
Hood: Six peacock herls, extended ¼ inch at hook eye
Originated by Paul Kukonen, Worcester, Massachusetts, one of the first to fish with shrimp flies

Skipping Bug
(*Striped bass and Florida species*)

Hook: No. 3/0, long shank
Tail: Bucktail, dyed yellow, 4 inches in length
Body: Balsa wood 1½ inches long, forward quarter painted red, remainder white (or blue with white)
Eye: Yellow with black center
Originated by Joe Brooks
Constructed by Bill Gallasch, Richmond, Virginia

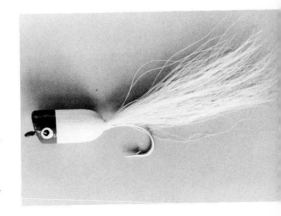

141

Bomber
(*Sailfish, amberjack*)

Hook: Nos. 5/0–7/0
Tail: Five or six broad white hackles with webby maraboulike fibers left on
Body: Dylite plastic (polystyrene), 1 inch diameter at face tapered to ⅜ inch at tail; overall length 1¼ inches (on 7/0 hook)
Eye: Small, red with black center
Bill Gallasch, Richmond, Virginia

Diving Popper
(*Striped bass and bluefish*)

Hook: No. 3/0, long shank
Tail: Yellow bucktail with three 1/64-inch Mylar strips intermingled
Hackle: Yellow
Body: 1-inch-long cork, tapered to hook eye, painted yellow
Eye: Black with white center
Dick Lohr, Stratford, Connecticut

Rock Crab
(*Striped bass*)

Hook: No. 1/0
Tail: Brown bucktail, 1 inch long
Body: Clipped deer hair
Hackle: Furnace-tied palmer
Hood: Brown bucktail, stubs protruding over hook eye
Head: Black
Ron Montecalvo, Providence, Rhode Island

Bub's Sand Eel
(*Striped bass*)

Hooks: No. 1/0 (two)
Thread: Red
Body: Hooks in tandem using 30-pound leader
    material, 4-inch Mylar tubing covering, with
    forward hook point through tubing
Tail: ¼-inch Mylar strands unraveled from
    tubing
Wing: Two 4-inch badger saddle hackles tied
    down at tail
Throat: Eight long peacock sword strands
Bub Church, Plainfield, New Jersey

Hamada Silversides
(*Striped bass*)

Hook: No. 2, long shank
Body: Balsa wood covered with silver Mylar
    tubing and soaked in epoxy
Wing: White bucktail next to body with lav-
    ender and green over, in that order, tied at
    tail and coated with clear epoxy
Tail: Continuation of bucktail from wing, free-
    flowing
Hal Janssen, Lafayette, California

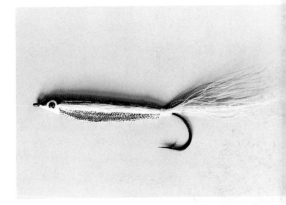

No-Name Tandem Streamer
(*Albacore, yellowtail, barracuda, and shark*)

Hooks: No. 2, tandem
Thread: Red
Tail: Purple over white bucktail
Body: Hooks in tandem and silver Mylar tubing
Wing: Purple over white bucktail 4½ inches
    long, with one grizzly saddle hackle flat on
    top; four strands of peacock herl over all
Head: Red, ⅜ inch long
Allan Rohrer, Long Beach, California

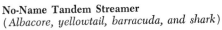

Sea-Arrow Squid

(*Striped bass, shark, grouper, and albacore*)

Hook: No. 3/0, XL shank

Tail: Ten white neck hackles 2½ inches long, flared outward in all directions; two 4½-inch white saddle hackles (as tentacles, one on each side)

Cheeks: Few strands of purple bucktail and short white marabou

Eyes: 8 mm flat amber glass

Body: Large-size white chenille over heavily padded base, tapered to hook eye

Fin (optional): White acrylic yarn, four 1-inch strands tied in middle, behind hook eye, soaked with lacquer, and trimmed to arrowhead shape

Note: May also be tied in red, brown, blue, pink, or yellow

Bob Edgley and Dan Blanton, San Jose, California

Jetty Bug

(*Spotted and sand bass, perch, and bonito*)

Hook: Nos. 4–8, 3XL shank

Tail: Two olive-green-dyed hackle quills, stripped

Body: Weighted, covered with dark-green chenille (optional fluorescent red chenille under belly to appear as series of spots)

Shell case: Olive-green rayon ribbon (4,000-denier viscose rayon)

Legs: Olive-green saddle hackle, palmered

Antennae: Same as tail

Head: Black

John F. McKim, Long Beach, California

Hooks and
Materials

Hooks

Owing to the corrosive nature of salt water, the hooks used in tying salt water flies must be made of rustproof metals.

Z-Nickel and Duranickel are nonrusting nickel alloys that are completely unaffected by salt water. However, nickel hooks are not quite as hard as those of the usual tempered steel which we use in fresh water. To compensate for this, hooks made of nickel alloys are usually of heavier wire than a steel hook of the same size. This, of course, increases the sink rate of the fly, and the hook point, being a little softer, can become dulled more readily. Using a hook hone occasionally will remedy this.

By far the most popular hooks in use for salt water fishing are those made of stainless steel. These are not at all affected by salt water. They are second in strength only to the best tempered-steel hooks and hold the point sharpness equally as well.

You will also find tin-plated hooks, but these have the obvious drawback of susceptibility to rust, particularly when the hook point is sharpened and the plating is removed thereby. Some tyers like them despite this, since they are available in lighter weights, which are desirable for some fishing conditions.

Tying Threads

Through the years, silk thread has been a standard tying material. However, silk does not stand up in salt water. Fortunately for fly tyers, threads composed of synthetics have been developed that are more durable. They are used by tyers in all areas.

Some years ago, fly tyers began to run across thread known as monocord, a multi-filament nylon thread with only a slight twist. It seemed to have all of the features required for a tying thread and has worked well for salt water flies. It is quite strong and it lies flat in the tying procedure, both attributes being desirable to the tyer.

The correspondence received in the course of our research contains frequent references to this thread, and quite a few flies illustrated have been tied with it.

Tinsel

Here is an outstanding example of a space-age material that has come to the aid of the tyer of salt water flies.

The conventional metal-silver tinsel used for many years by fresh water tyers tarnishes after its first dip in salt water. However, space-age technology has come up with Mylar, a polyester plastic which is metallic in appearance but is absolutely nontarnishing. It is available in tinsel form, in the 1/32-inch and 1/64-inch widths which are most popular for use in wrapping bodies and adding strips for flash. In addition, some inquisitive fly tyer discovered a millinery material known as Mylar piping, which is constructed by braiding Mylar strands into a hollow tube. This gained immediate popularity as a body for streamer flies, and you will find this illustrated in the tying of the streamers.

If you keep an eye on the gift wrap counters during holiday seasons, you will find Mylar cords (or piping) in various colors used for gift wrapping. The fine diameters are very useful in wrapping bodies, with the inner cord removed. This makes a more satisfactory wrapped body, since it is more durable than the tinsel, which may be nicked by the tooth of a fish and become unwrapped, to say nothing of the same thing happening on a back-cast.

Other Materials

Without a doubt, the bucktail fly is considered the most durable type of construction.

You will have noted in the preceding fly tying sequences that the basic construction of salt water streamers and bucktails includes the use of hair, primarily bucktail (or you may use polar bear, if you have any left), and hackles, all of different colors and sizes.

Saddle and neck hackles are used in two different ways in the construction of streamers, in many cases being tied to trail behind the hook, giving the appearance of length as well as an undulating action. They are also used as a hackle or collar, when wrapped around the hook shank to create a different illusion.

Other materials shown in the tying sequences include chenille and wool or nylon yarns, as well as marabou, peacock herl, nylon hair, and jungle cock body feathers and nail feathers, the last being quite scarce due to import restrictions.

To finish off the fly and seal the thread on the head of the fly, you will want fly tying cement or lacquer. At present, epoxy cement is the ultimate as a sealant to protect exposed threads on any part of the fly. This cement is practically indestructible and, if obtained in the crystal clear grade, does a great deal in bringing out the thread colors. (See Mark Sosin and the Blockbuster.)

Refer to your favorite dealers in fly tying materials, since most of the foregoing items have common application in all fly tying procedures and are not limited to salt water use.

A Word on Tackle

To acquaint you with salt water tackle in general use today by fly rodders, we have summarized the preferences of the experienced fishermen with whom we corresponded.

Rods

The most popular rod is a two-piece, 9-foot, six-ounce glass rod, preferably with a slow action. There are some who prefer a longer 9½-foot rod, citing its greater ability to pick the line up from the water. Others prefer a shorter 8½-foot fly rod, and they have their reasons too.

In examining the standards set up by the salt water fly rod makers, we note that their average models are in the 9-foot to 9½-foot range, the larger size being classified as heavy duty and recommended largely for offshore game fishing.

Fly Lines

Fly lines are classified as floating (F), sinking (S), and sinking tip (F/S), all in combination with various tapers.

Your first salt water fly line should be a floating line, and the weight of this line should be based on the rod of your choice. It is best that you buy your rod, reel, and line at the same time and from a reliable tackle dealer.

Above the handle of the rod, the maker indicates the recommended weight of line to use with the rod. This might be anywhere from No. 9 to No. 11, depending on the action of the rod.

Your next consideration is the taper to be selected. Look for the Weight Forward (WF) lines which include the Salt Water Taper, specially designed to allow for less false casting and to permit you to present your fly to a moving fish within a minimum time. This can be all important, and may mean the difference between giving the fish a look at your fly or not.

So let us say that you need a No. 10 floating line to match your rod. Ask your tackle dealer for a WF10F—Salt Water Taper fly line. Sinking lines present a problem for the fresh water fisherman learning to cast in salt water, for the timing required to pick up the line from the water is different. Without a stripping basket the retrieved line sinks faster in the water and is pulled away by the tide.

Consequently, for your transition to salt water fly casting you should practice with the floating line before actually fishing.

The lead core "shooting head," which is in great use on the West Coast today, also has its place in fly rodding, especially for long-distance casting, and is another step to which you will advance later.

Fly Line Backing

Fly line backing is a small diameter line of known breaking strength which is put on the spool of the reel first and spliced to the fly line. The amount of backing should be no less than 100 yards and can possibly amount to 250 to 300 yards for big game fishing.

Braided dacron lines available for other fishing purposes are recommended, and the breaking strength to be selected should be greater than the tippet strength. Hence, a 15- to 18-pound backing will be quite satisfactory for a start.

Leaders

As in fresh water fly fishing, tapered leaders are recommended. Ready-made tapered leaders can be purchased from your tackle dealer. However, it is recommended that the leader be of hard nylon for maximum stiffness. This stiffness is more important for salt water casting, to aid in the "turn over" of the heavier flies you will be using. The tippet strength of the leader should be no less than 12 pounds. This is the most practical tippet strength in use today.

You may wish to tie your own leaders, in which case a popular formula would be four feet of 30-pound hard nylon, to which you tie two feet of 25-pound, one foot of 20-pound, one foot of 15-pound, and then the tippet of at least one foot of 12-pound. The tippet will then conform to most tournament regulations, if you wish to enter a fish for record.

A wire shock leader is necessary when fishing for bluefish, which can cut through the tippet, or for tarpon. A heavy 40- to 100-pound nylon tippet, one foot long, is advisable.

Reels

Salt water fly fishing reels are more than just a place to store your line, as is often the case in fresh water fishing.

Choose a reel large enough to hold the fly line as well as at least 200 yards of backing, one built of nonrust metals light in weight, and of sturdy construction. The drag, which is most important, can be the difference between boating your fish or losing it. Reels on the market today that are classified for salt water use incorporate these features, with the one variable usually being the quality of the drag. Here you will have latitude in chosing the reel suitable for your fishing conditions. For example, the requirements for drag would be greater for tarpon than if you were going after striped bass.

Your reel should be selected with the advice of your tackle dealer. Tell him what fishing you will be doing. In general, you are going to get what you pay for: quality and pricing of reels are closely related.

Reels available today come in single action, where the handle is generally fastened to the spool, or in multiplying action, where a gear ratio is employed so that each turn of the handle turns the spool twice or more. The multiplying reel offers the advantage of quicker retrieve of slack line. This is a valuable feature. If you are record minded, however, check the rules of any tournament you wish to enter. The current Salt Water Fly Rodders of America rules forbid the use of a multiplying reel for a fly-caught entry.